Korean Royal Palace
Changdeokgung

Korean Royal Palace : Changdeokgung

Text · Illustration : Yi Hyang-woo
Translation : Won Hyeon-suk, Yi Choonsun
Supervision : Na Gak-sun, Mark Patton
Photograph : Heo Kyong-hee, Yi Hyang-woo

Published : January 30, 2015
Second edition : July 20, 2016
Published by : INMUNWALK Publishing Co.
Publisher : Heo Kyong-hee

Address : Address : 401Ho, 445-4, Hoedong-gil, Paju-si, Gyeonggi-do, Korea, 10881
E-mail : inmunwalk@naver.com
Telephone No. : 82-31-949-9792
Facsimile No. : 82-31-949-9793
Registration of Publishing : September 1, 2009

ISBN 978-89-98259-05-1   03910

This book has been funded to be translated by Publication Industry Promotion Agency
of Korea.

This book's CIP of the National library of Korea is able to use through 'http://seoji.nl.go.kr'
and 'http://www.nl.go.kr/kolisnet'.(CIP No. : CIP2015002138)

Korean Royal Palace
Changdeokgung

Text · Illustration   Yi Hyang-woo
Translation   Won Hyeon-suk, Yi Choonsun
Supervision   Na Gak-sun, Mark Patton

INMUNWALK

Contents

1

A Road to
Donhwamun Gate

Would you stop for a moment around the flower garden from across the street and have a distant view of the commanding figure of Donhwamun Gate?

The way to Donhwamun Gate
from Jongno 3(sam)-ga Street

I am going to take a rather different approach to Changdeokgung (昌德宮) Palace from the conventional way that one gets off at Anguk Station of Seoul Subway line 3 and walks to the palace. If you start from Jongno 3(sam)-ga Street Station of Subway line 1 or 5, you can get a better perspective of Donhwamun Gate all the while you walk northward toward Changdeokgung Palace.

Seen from the south along the Donhwamun Street, Donhwamun Gate appears to have Eungbong Peak on its top.

Scenes of Donhwamunno Street from Jongno 3(sam)-ga Street to Changdeokgung Palace

Walking along somewhat quiet Donhwamunno Street now makes you feel better than it did when the street used to be crowded with people lining up in front of the box offices of two movie theaters such as Danseongsa and Picadilly Cinema. Moreover, approaching the palace this way, you can have a better view of Donhwamun Gate with the distant Eungbong Peak on its top as the backdrop.

It would be also good to visualize the street of ministry offices that used to be there in front of Changdeokgung Palace in the past. Even after Gyeongbokgung Palace was destroyed and left in ruins after the Japanese Invasion in 1592, the Street of Six

Changdeokgung Palace, a UNESCO World Heritage

View of Changdeokgung Palace

Ministries in front of Gyeongbokgung continued to function. Meanwhile, smaller government office buildings got naturally clustered along the street in front of Donhwamun Gate as Changdeokgung Palace was practically performing the role as the primary palace for the last half of the Joseon Dynasty. There are sites of government offices like *Jongbusi* (Office in charge of publishing the Royal lineage and inspection of the Royal relatives), *Tongnyewon* (Office in charge of rituals such as audiences and ancestral ceremonies), and *Bibyeonsa* (The highest administrative office, the Border Defense Council of Joseon) as well as Ehwa Hoegwan Building which accommodates the Jeonju Lee Royal Family Association.

12

Donhwamun Gate and
its Stone Foundation *Woldae*

At last, the main gate of Changdeokgung Palace, Donhwamun
(敦化門) reveals itself across the street. If the traffic signal has not
changed to green, you may take advantage of the time to look
around the flower beds and have a view of the commanding
figure of Donhwamun Gate. Now, we get to cross the street and
go near the gate. There is a long wall to the right, and we can
see the trees and roofs of the palace buildings beyond the wall.

Donhwamun Gate (Treasure No. 383)

The restored *woldae* and *Sanguiwon* compound

They belonged to *Sanguiwon* which was the office that kept the king's clothing and the royal family's valuables and ornaments.

After you reach the main gate of Changdeokgung Palace, Donhwamun, would you stop and pay attention to the spacious stone foundation called *woldae* in front of the gate? The gate is a little bit elevated on the *woldae* which is higher than ground level and has some steps at the south end. People are rarely aware that there exists such *woldae* except that they just regard it as a meeting place or a picture spot before they get in the palace.

The *woldae* and the threshold of Donhwamun Gate had been

buried in the early 1900s so that Emperor Sunjong's vehicle could pass through the gate easily. He took his car when he paid a visit to Deoksugung Palace to ask after his father, the abdicated Emperor Gojong.

However, the imperfect restoration of the *woldae* leaves much regret because it does not look as imposing as before but rather awkward. The restored *woldae* is not as high as it used to be since the asphalt paved street has become much higher for a long period than the *woldae* is. The section connecting Jongmyo Shrine and Changdeokgung Palace is currently being restored along the Yulgongno Street. We expect that the street in front of Donhwamun Gate will also be refurbished more naturally by the time the restoration is completed.

Shall we now purchase an admission ticket and enter Changdeokgung Palace? People had to join a guided tour according to their language and designated time to see the palace buildings before. However, since it is not compulsory anymore now, you are free to look around and enjoy on your own even though you will need some preliminary knowledge about the palace. In such a case, you can buy the guidebook at the ticket office, but you do not have to rely too much on the general chronological information which anyone else can get on the internet.

Donhwamunno Street seen from the *woldae*

From now on, what you choose to see and what kind of impression you want to get depend on your personal taste. If you want to enjoy a more cozy atmosphere, it would be better for you to arrive at the palace earlier in the morning hours. You should also know that choosing to visit the palace in bad weather conditions can sometimes give you an opportunity to have an unexpectedly wonderful tour. As the conventional wisdom is that touring the palace is a picnic on a fine day, they mostly tend to pick a crowded day.

However, if you dare to visit the palace on a rainy day when everything gets moistened, you can see the more tranquil and deepened colors of the palace. Changdeokgung Palace is a specially attractive place that can touch you in a different way depending upon the season, the weather, and the time from dawn to dusk. On a cloudy day the palace looks like a monotone sketch, and walking on a clear moonlit night you cannot but fall in love with it. How about beginning your own special excursion to Changdeokgung from now?

2

Crossing
Geumcheongyo Bridge

Geumhomun

Geumcheongyo

Jinseonmun

Donhwamun

The *Painting of the Eastern Palaces* : the vicinity of Geumcheongyo Bridge

Changdeokgung Palace also Known as the Eastern Palace

'Changdeok' means 'to let virtues prosper.' Changdeokgung is one of the five palaces (Gyeongbokgung, Changdeokgung, Changgyeonggung, Gyeonghuigung, Gyeongungung-current Deoksugung). King Taejo who founded the Joseon Dynasty in 1392 moved the capital to Hanyang (present Seoul) in 1394, and built Gyeongbokgung as the primary palace. Changdeokgung was built in 1405 (the 5th year of the third king Taejo) as a ✿ secondary palace. It was built at the foot of Eungbong Peak, and the buildings were arranged with the topography taken into consideration.

Changgyeonggung was also built next to it so that the residential area of Changdeokgung could be extended. Changgyeonggung was built at the site of the former Suganggung Palace, where King Taejong lived after he abdicated the throne

✿ **Secondary Palace** : While the primary palace was where the king mainly lived and took care of the affairs of state, the secondary palaces were spare ones that the king needed to move to in case there were problems due to fires, diseases, and other personal or political situations.

A milestone marking Changdeokgung as a World Heritage Site

in favor of son King Sejong. Changgyeonggung was especially built as the residences for three queen dowagers during the reign of King Seongjong, who were Queen Jeonghui (Queen of King Sejo), Queen Sohye (Queen of King Deokjong), and Queen Ansun (Queen of King Yejong). The Rear Garden was shared by Changdeokgung and Changgyeonggung, and as they were located to the east of Gyeongbokgung, they were collectively called the Eastern Palaces.

After all the palaces were burnt down during the Japanese Invasion of 1592 to 1598, Changdeokgung was rebuilt by Prince Gwanghaegun in 1610 and had been used as the virtual primary palace of the Joseon Dynasty for about 270 years. Then after

Gyeonghuigung Palace was built, it was also called the Western Palace. Since Gyeongbokgung was rebuilt during the reign of King Gojong, Changdeokgung had remained vacant from 1894 to 1907. When Emperor Sunjong was enthroned in November of 1907, he moved into Changdeokgung Palace, however, it soon became the last scene of the Joseon Dynasty due to the forced annexation by Japan in 1910.

Among the rear gardens of the remaining Joseon Palaces, only that of Changdeokgung has been well preserved, and shows how the architecture and the natural scenery are making superb harmony with each other. Acknowledged for retaining characteristics and beauty of Korean traditional landscaping, Changdeokgung including the Rear Garden has been enlisted as a UNESCO World Heritage since 1997. The entire area encompassed by Changdeokgung is about 120 acres (480,340m²), of which the Rear Garden occupies roughly two thirds (297,520m²).

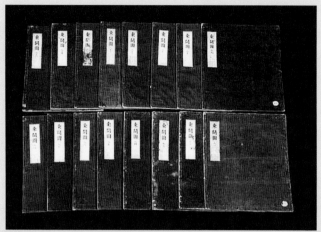

The *Painting of the Eastern Palaces*, a set of 16 picture map albums

❖ **The *Painting of the Eastern Palaces*** : This is a set of 16 picture map albums. Two sets remain, and one of them is kept in the Korea University Museum while the other one is in the Dong-A University Museum. The one at Korea University is made in a series of 16-page picture map albums. Each album contains six page maps that are linked vertically. The other one at the Dong-A University museum is made in the form of a folding picture screen. It is thought that the one at Korea University is the original form. Its cover is mounted with thin blue cloth, and the title, *Painting of the Eastern Palaces*, Vol. 1 to Vol. 16 of the Set '人 (Human)', is written on a small long rectangular white silk cloth framed with red paper. We can surmise that three sets of the map, '天 (Heaven),' '地 (Earth),' and '人 (Human)' were originally made. Each picture map is painted on a piece of silk cloth 36.5centimeter wide and 45.5centimeter long. Six page maps are linked to form a vertically unfoldable album. When these 16 albums are horizontally connected, they make up one set, which is 576centimeter wide and 273centimeter long as a whole.

The *Painting of the Eastern Palaces* employed a bird's-eye view, and minutely depicts Changdeokgung and Changgyeonggung surrounded with mountains and hills, not only in black ink but also in color. This is an excellent artwork painted with masterful techniques by painters of *Dohwaseo* (the Royal Bureau of Painting). This map illustrates the contents as described in *Gunggwolji* (Book of Palaces) with more accuracy adding a three dimensional effect to them. To paint the mountains and hills, the Southern School technique of Chinese painting (南宗画: *nanzhonghua*), often called "literati painting (文人画: *wenrenhua*)" was used, but in describing the buildings in detail and giving the perspective to the painting, western techniques also had influence. However, rather than as rather than as just artwork, this set, this set of picture maps is more significant as a vivid resource for research in that it helps get hold of what the original layout was like including buildings, facilities, and landscaping. Furthermore, it is highly valuable as a historical resource to restore the damaged or missing structures to their original form of the 19th century.

The *Painting of the Eastern Palaces* is presumed to have been made around 1824~1830. Gyeongbokjeon Hall of Changdeokgung, which was burned in 1824 (the 24th year of King Sunjo), is depicted as an empty site only. Some halls in Changgyeonggung such as Hwangyeongjeon, Gyeongchunjeon, and Yanghwadang which were burned by fires in 1830 are painted in the map. These facts allow us to assume that the painting was made during the period after the fire in August of 1824 and before the fire in 1830. The structure of Yeongyeongdang Hall painted in the map is different from that of the present Yeongyeongdang which was built in 1828. The structure of the present Yeongyeongdang rather coincides with another anonymous building painted on the top right side of the painting. From these facts, it is possible to assume that the painting was made before 1827 prior to constructing the present Yeongyeongdang. Otherwise, Yeongyeongdang could have been constructed in the same shape as depicted in the picture map, and have been rebuilt in the present shape during the reign of King Heonjong. Nevertheless, the assumption is still lingering that the anonymous building in the top right might be the Yeongyeongdang which could have been constructed right after the painting was made or during the period while it was being made.

The *Painting of the Eastern Palaces*, made around 1830, National Treasure No. 249
(Korea University Museum collection)

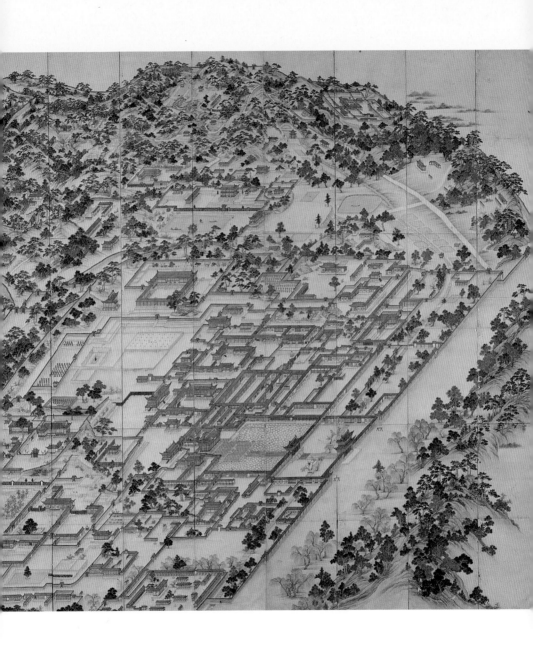

Old pagoda trees in the palace yard seem to hug
and greet the visitors.

Shall we now look into the palace yard in detail?

Donhwamun gate was first built in the 12th year of King Taejong (1412) as the main gate of Changdeokgung Palace. However, since it was burned during the Japanese Invasion of 1592 to 1598, it was reconstructed in 1608 when Prince Gwanghaegun was enthroned. Donhwamun is the oldest among the existing gates of the Joseon palaces. 'Donhwa (敦化)' originated

Donhwamun Gate seen from inside the palace yard

from the phrase 'daedeok donhwa (大德敦化)' in the *Doctrine of the Mean* (中庸 : *Zhōng yōng*), which means 'The king governs with warm heart and edifies people with virtues.'

On the second floor of Donhwamun Gate, there were a bell and a drum to inform people of time and any emergency. At ✿ *injeong*, they tolled the bell, and at ✿*paru*, they beat the drum. Donhwamun Gate was used by the king or Chinese envoys, and especially by the officials of the Office of Inspector General. There is also an article in *King Yeongjo's Annals* that he received a ceremony that offered a rebel leader's head on the upper story after rebel forces were suppressed in the fourth year reign of his in 1728. Oh! My! How awful it is to imagine the scene when they hung the head of the rebellion's leader on the gate!

Inside Donhwamun Gate

✿ *Paru* and *Injeong* : The Joseon Dynasty enforced a curfew in Hanyang (current Seoul). Signalling the curfew around 10 p.m. was called *injeong*. To wish for a peaceful night, they tolled the bell 28 times because it was believed among East Asian countries that there are Twenty-Eight Mansions in the sky (二十八宿 Èr Shí Bā Xiù), as part of Chinese Confucian astronomy. *Paru* means to beat the drum 33 times to announce lifting the curfew. Both *injeong* and *paru* started from the Water Pavilion of the palace, and were relayed to Belfry, Sungnyemun Gate (South Gate), and Heunginjimun Gate (East Gate), one after another. Then all four gates of the city were closed with the sound. After *injeong*, patrolmen pounded a beat with a wooden clapper. *Injeong* was announced by tolling the iron bell as metal belongs to *yin* corresponding to 'night' and 'sleep.' On the contrary, *paru* was announced by beating the drum made of wood, which belongs to yang and corresponds to 'day' and 'doing activities.' However, when they suffered from drought, they tolled the bell even at *paru* in the early morning to boost *yin* energy to call in rainfall. When the drought got severe, the South Gate representing yang was closed, and the North Gate meaning *yin* energy was opened instead, as they thought 'water' and 'north' correspond to *yin*. However, throughout the Joseon Dynasty, as droughts repeatedly occurred, such a practice got almost routinized that distinguishing *injeong* from *paru* with the bell and the drum lost its original meaning, and had disappeared gradually.

Ogo meant beating the drum at 12 o'clock noon. When the soldier on duty announced *ogo* in the center of the palace, the king and all the other people in the palace wrapped up the morning work, and got ready to have lunch.

Geumhomun, Yogeummun, and Danbongmun

Geumhomun Gate is the west gate of Changdeokgung. 'Geumho' literally means 'metal tiger.' According to the five elements, metal corresponds to the west, and the *White Tiger* is the guardian deity in charge of the west. While the officials of the Office of the Inspector General could pass through the main gate Donhwamun, the rest of the officials used the west gate

Geumhomun Gate

Yogeummun Gate

Danbongmun Gate

Geumhomun as most of their quarters were located right inside the Geumhomun Gate.

We can see the Yogeummun Gate on our way out from the Rear Garden (Secret Garden) tour. Queen Inhyeon was driven out of the palace through this gate carried in a white palanquin after having been deposed from her position. It was also through this gate that she entered when she was later reinstated as queen.

A small gate along the southern wall is Danbongmun Gate which was used mainly by the court ladies and the royal relatives including the in-law of the royal family.

Now, it is time that we looked into the palace yard in detail. When you enter Donhwamun Gate, you can see some old pagoda trees that are designated as a Natural Monument of Korea. Planting pagoda trees in the palace originated from the legend that the prime minister and two vice premiers of the ancient Zhou Dynasty took care of state affairs while being seated under pagoda trees.

Pagoda trees often called Chinese scholar trees

Naebyeongjo and *Sanguiwon* area across Geumcheongyo Bridge

If you turn your eyes to the other side of Geumcheongyo Bridge, to the south is a restricted area designated for the maintenance office of the palace. However, we feel like peeping into the area as it is especially beautiful when winter plums and Korean cherry flowers are in full bloom in the spring.

There used to be *Naebyeongjo*, the military facilities inside the palace, and to the right was *Sangbang*. *Sangbang* also known as *Sanguiwon* was an office that prepared clothing for the king and safekept treasures and ornaments. At present, the building of *Naebyeongjo* is being used by the Changdeokgung Palace Office.

Pagoda trees in full swing of vernal greenery inside Donhwamun

Zelkova trees in full glory of golden autumn leaves
by Geumcheongyo Bridge

Geumcheongyo, the Forbidden Bridge over Silky Water

Around here, it may be helpful to take a look at the guide map of Changdeokgung. If you take a few more steps, on the opposite side of Geumhomun Gate appears an elaborately decorated stone bridge. It is a forbidden bridge called Geumcheongyo, laid over a waterway, which artificially induces water into the front part of the palace to make more auspicious

Geumcheongyo Bridge in the autumn

39

the palace already standing against the backdrop of the mountain according to Korean geomantic theory, *pungsu* (風水 : feung shui).

Geumcheongyo Bridge of Changdeokgung is the oldest stone bridge among the forbidden bridges of the Joseon Dynasty. It was constructed by Bak Ja-cheong in the 11th year of King Taejong (1411). In all the outer court areas of palaces was dug a forbidden stream so that it could not only prohibit any trespassers from entering the palace but also make officials purify and straighten their mind before taking care of the state affairs.

Geumcheongyo in Changdeokgung literally means a bridge

A turtle laid at the north side of the arches of Geumcheongyo Bridge

Baektaek and *nati* on the south side
of Geumcheongyo Bridge

Baektaek on the south side of Geumcheongyo Bridge

over silky water. To your regret, the waterway being now cut off, we cannot see the silky water that used to flow under the bridge. If you come on a rainy day, you may be able to merely taste the mood of the old days.

Standing under the tall zelkova tree, and looking under the bridge, you can see the bridge is built on two arches. The balustrades are elaborately decorated with lotus leaf patterns and eye-shaped openings. Stone statues built on the balusters and between the arches symbolize warning. The turtle laid between the arches on the north side is the *Black Tortoise*, which is a guardian deity in charge of the north, and *baektaek* on the south side is a mythological auspicious animal symbolizing the advent of a sage king. In addition, the fierce looking devil called *nati* is engraved in an inverted triangular

41

Peach trees in full blossom by Geumcheongyo Bridge

shape on both sides of the bridges to ward off any bad energy that may come into the palace through the waterway.

One of the mythological auspicious stone animals, a *haechi* is also placed upon each newel post so that they may guard the palace, however, their facial expressions do not quite seem to be frightening or stern enough to undertake such grave duty. Some of them move their heads slantwise, and others look like they are grinning at us as if they feel very close and

A stone animal statue with its tail winding up

42

Stone animal statues with a variety of facial expressions engraved upon the newel posts of Geumcheongyo Bridge

friendly with us. Moreover, what about the light movement of the tail winding upward? Even the tail at the backside seems to be putting on an impish smile.

Only the stone mason who fully understood the attributes of granite could have had an easy and liberal mind to carve such sculptures. If any Italian sculptor made such loose sculptures, the works would have certainly been assessed as of less artistic value. The sculptures are made of rough and hard granite which was abundant in Joseon, and pecked out with a coarse chisel, truly manifesting the mature and relaxed attitude of Joseon masons.

Spring runs along the waterway under Geumcheongyo···

Shade of autumn flowing along the water under Geumcheongyo.

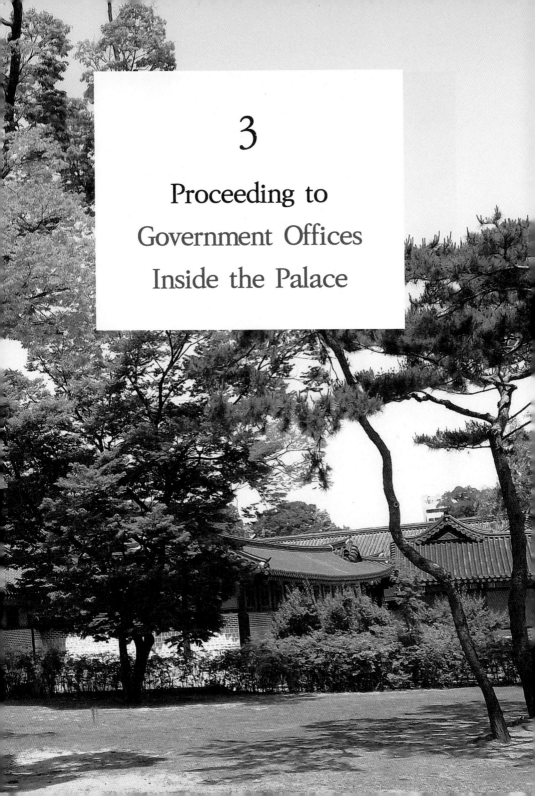

3

Proceeding to
Government Offices
Inside the Palace

Entering Naegak Pavilion, your eyes catch the vivid image
of the roof lines

Small Office Quarters Inside the Palace

Before you get into the inner core section of the palace, there are some places you should never miss on the tour. Those are the small office quarters unfolding themselves to the west, inside the walls of the Geumhomun Gate. They are collectively called *Gwolnaegaksa* (闕內各司 : Government Offices Inside the Palace), where you find the UNESCO milestone to the front.

Gwolnaegaksa was small office quarters for the court officials who carried out their business at the palace. It can be interpreted as the central government complex on the palace

In front of Naegak

precincts. While the big office quarters off the precincts called the Street of Six Ministries was lined along the street in front of the Gwanghwamun Gate, small office quarters were clustered inside the palace compound to assist the king from close at hand. *Gwolnaegaksa* demolished during the Japanese occupation was restored in 2005 and now looks just as it did back in the old days. Of course, it lacks time-honored class and its buildings look a little crude owing to recent restoration. However, no palace other than Changdeokgung had got its *Gwolnaegaksa* restored, which means a lot to Koreans. I would like you to put aside strange feelings from the newly-constructed buildings for now and to try to enjoy their intrinsic features as palace structures. A large swath of palace halls and pavilions were so damaged during Japanese rule that you are rather accustomed to seeing disconnected buildings and sparsely occupied compounds.

The original structure of palaces was one in which one building was connected to another with walls or with corridor buildings within a compound. Thus, you could not gain access to any building belonging to another compound without passing through its compound's gate. Now, the *Gwolnaegaksa* reconstructed in the western section of Changdeokgung has allowed you to follow the same moving paths as the Joseon people did. It can be so much fun and historically meaningful as well.

You may keep your eyes out at overlapping roof lines made

Name plaque of Naegak

by neighboring halls, passing through the narrow gate with your head lightly bowed. Watching the waterway flowing into the forbidden stream, you may cross the bridge looking for *maehwa* (winter plums) that are stealthily revealing themselves over the wall in early spring days. Also, even an autumn day when ginkgo trees shed their leaves may be remembered for its resplendent beauty.

When you enter *Gwolnaegaksa* with a commanding zelkova tree on your right, you will find the name plaque of the gate that reads Naegak (內閣). It is another name of the Gyujanggak (奎章閣) Office. King Jeongjo prepared for Gyujanggak officials an office-cum-night duty room, which was called Naegak.

51

Pass through the gate and turn right, and you will catch sight of good scenery such as the waterway to the east, the wall over it, and the overlapping roof lines beyond the wall. It is just one of the beautiful scenes you encounter in the *Gwolnaegaksa* compound. Overlapping and continuing roof lines in an ink black color against the blue sky are superb landscape drawings created

Geomseocheong

The view seen from Geomseocheong

by Korean traditional architecture, not to mention the rising curve (catenary line) at the roof ends. Passing through the next gate, you find the Geomseocheong Office (檢書廳 : Publication Office) located to the east of the Geumcheon Stream. The view seen from the building is lovely.

Geomseocheong was structure attached to the Gyujanggak Office and an office-cum night duty room for publication officials. King Jeongjo appointed four publication officials Seo I-su, Bak Je-ga, Yu Deuk-gong, and Yi Deok-mu in 1779. All of them were born out of wedlock and discriminated aggainst by recruiting government officials. Recruiting these four illegitimate children for the publication office was almost unprecedented at the time even though they were invested with the very low rank of junior seventh degree(7B) usually belonging to military officials. They stood for night duty without a proper room to spend the night in. At first they were standing by at a back room of the Gyujanggak Office and got their own office of Geomseocheong in 1783 when it was built as an annex to Gyujanggak.

When you pass through the small gate of Geomseocheong and turn left, you will catch sight of Gyujanggak (奎章閣) Office . In the year King Jeongjo ascended the throne (1776), the king established an archive for storing writings and calligraphic works of successive kings. The archive was a two-story building, and its first floor was named Gyujanggak Library and its second floor Juhamnu (宙合樓) Pavilion. Then an office under the immediate control of the library was built to the west of the building. However, the office had such a secluded location that its officials felt it

Wicket door leading to Gyujanggak from Geomseocheor

was very inconvenient. Thus it was moved to the *Gwolnaegaksa* compound in the fifth year of King Jeongjo's rule (1781). The *Hangyeongjiryak* (漢京誌略 : a history book on old Seoul during the Joseon dynasty) contained a description about the Gyujanggak Office: "King Jeongjo wrote its name plaque in person···. The king

Gyujanggak Office

presented silver cups, an ink stone, a Korean lute, a Korean mandolin, a jar for arrow throwing, and six jade lamps to the office. The office has all these gifts hung on the beams and a brass rain gauge placed in its yard. The Gyujanggak Library office is the largest and widest space of all the palace buildings."

King Jeongjo built another archive on Ganghwado Island in the sixth year of his reign (1782) with a view to keeping royal documents and named the new archive ✿Outer Gyujanggak (外奎章 閣). Then the king called the first archive Inner Gyujanggak (內奎章 閣) and used both archives to keep important royal publications, completing the Inner and the Outer Gyujanggak system.

✿ *Collection of Outer Gyujanggak* (外奎章閣 圖書, *les manuscrits coréens*)∶ During the French campaign against Korea (丙寅洋擾 in 1866) Admiral Rose, commander of the French Far Eastern Fleet, landed on Ganghwado Island and bombarded the archive building. As a result, some 5,000 volumes of books were burned, and lots of silver bars and 340 volumes of historical books including *Uigwe* (儀軌∶ Joseon Royal Court Protocols) were looted. In 1993 President Mitterrand of France visited Korea to win an order for TGV's high-speed railway network, returning one volume of *Uigwe*. The President promised to return the whole *collection of Outer Gyujanggak*, but the two countries were not able to find common ground. Then at the G20 Summit held in Seoul in 2010, The Korean President accepted a permanent lease agreement on a 5-year renewal basis. Eventually, in May, 2011, in entire collection was retrieved 145 years later. It was regrettable in that we could not demand full ownership of the royal books, but it was also historically significant in that we could recover our cultural assets which were illegitimately smuggled out.

✿ **Dr. Park Byeong-seon**∶ The *Collection of Outer Gyujanggak* housed in the Bibliothèque nationale de France (National Library of France) revealed its existence to the world through the efforts of the late Park Byeong-seon (1928~2011). When Ms. Park worked as a librarian of the French national library in 1972, she discovered the second volume of *Jikji* (a Korean Buddhist document published in 1377) and proved it was the world's oldest extant book printed with movable metal type. Afterwards, she found out the collection with rigorous efforts in 1978 and played a major role in repatriating the whole collection.

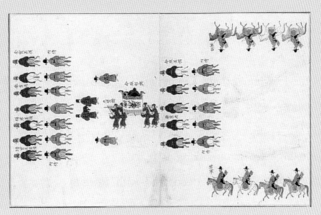

Banchado

✿ *Uigwe* (儀軌, Joseon Royal Court Protocols): This refers to Joseon books recording the details of royal rites on weddings, funerals, banquets, investiture, and coronation. From the very beginning of the dynasty *Uigwe* began to be published, but all of them were destroyed during the Japanese Invasion of the 16th century. Since the mid-Joseon dynasty, *Uigwe* was produced in full scale. The oldest extant one is about the funeral of Queen Uiin in 1601. In the 19th century the number of *Uigwe* increased and their quality improved. Tools and buildings that are hard to describe in words were recorded in drawings. The relative rank charts called *Banchado* (班次圖) were painted in vivid natural colors.

Bongmodang Hall and Juniper Tree

After looking around Gyujanggak, your next destination will be Bongmodang (奉謨堂) Hall, north of Geomseocheong. The Unhanmun (雲漢門) Gate leading to Bongmodang is placed on a set of steps and its wall is decorated with Korean Cherry trees planted in plenty in the front. In the late spring you can see white cherry petals fluttering all over, which gives the unique and refreshing flavor

Lock and iron door ring of the Unhanmun Gate

Unhanmun Gate and Bongmodang Hall

of spring days. Bongmodang was an archive where the articles left by successive kings were kept and 'bongmo (奉謨)' means treasuring up former kings' teachings as stern admonition. King Jeongjo moved writings, paintings, calligraphic works and letters of appointment of successive kings to a building in the Rear Garden and named the building Bongmodang. The current Bongmodang served the same function as the old one in the Rear Garden since 1857 (the 8th year of King Cheoljong's rule) as the Gyujanggak Library was scaled down after King Jeonjo's death. Its book collection was transferred to Jangseogak (藏書閣) Archive at Changgyeonggung Palace in 1969.

On the edge of the road between Bongmodang and the Royal stack room an imposing juniper tree is standing. The juniper tree (Korean Natural Monument No. 194) is assumed to be 750 years old. The tree was as tall as six meters, but it got its upper limb' broken down by a typhoon in September 2010. Still, the overall appearance that it forces out a loud belch remains commanding and majestic.

Juniper tree

Walking Along the Forbidden Stream

Walk along the Forbidden Stream looking towards the right, you will encounter a different partitioning of the site from that of the inner core section. The surrounding walls of Eokseongnu (憶昔樓) Pavilion and the Old Seonwonjeon Complex (舊璿源殿) block your field of vision. If you look over the walls, however, overlapping roof lines composed of the eastern section buildings including Injeongjeon Hall will wow you. Also, you will find the

A pavilion over the Forbidden Stream

Spring on the eastern wall

waterway of the Forbidden Stream and a petit pavilion over the stream. (Beware!! Watch your head. The doors around here are so low that you may bump your head against it, while walking distracted by awesome scenery.)

Before getting inside the Old Seonwonjeon Complex, why don't you stand on the bridge against the ginkgo tree, and have some time looking back over the path you just walked along? A book storage building and a grand ginkgo tree attract a lot of attention. The book storage is just a storage of a simple rectangular shape. However, the simple structure of the western wall and the long storage building reveal unique refinement and make you feel strangely comfortable when you stand in its front

Autumn on the eastern wall

yard.

When you look out to the north of the Old Seonwonjeon from the bridge, you will find a big building standing all by itself in the center of the pine grove. The building is called the Uipunggak (儀豊閣) Warehouse. It is assumed to have been constructed during Japanese rule and served as a warehouse to store articles owned by the royal household.

North of Old Seonwonjeon, Gyeongbokjeon (景福殿) Hall used to be located. The *Painting of the Eastern Palaces* marks the hall as the Gyeongbokjeon Site. That is, Gyeongbokjeon was already gone around the time when the *Painting of the Eastern Palaces*

Book storage   Uipunggak Warehouse

was completed. The hall was destroyed by fire in 1824 (the 24th year of King Sunjo's reign). West of Gyeongbokjeon lies Yeongmodang (永慕堂) Hall which was the residence of Dowager Inwon, the third wife of King Sukjong. Gyeongbokjeon was occupied by Dowager Jeongsun, the second wife of King Yeongjo. The whole district where Uipunggak is now standing was the compound dedicated to queen dowagers and it was also equipped with kitchen facilities for them.

Leave the storage, cross the bridge, pass through the big gate, and get into the walled compound. Then you will feel nice and cosy mainly because the walls embrace the whole space. The view over Geomseocheong and Bongmodang from this compound does not look the same as the one from there. Interestingly, different perspectives provide you with dissimilar impressions of the same building. On the southern corridor

Getting into the walled section, you find Jeongsukmun Gate and Eokseongnu Pavilion

Roofs of Yangjidang and Injeongjeon are seen over the Bochunmun Gate

building of Old Seonwonjeon stands a two-story building, Eokseongnu Pavilion. The *Hangyeongjiryak* said King Yeongjo ordered the Royal Pharmacy to observe rituals for ✿Shennong (神農) with his spirit tablet enshrined, and bestowed a four-letter writing '入審憶昔.' Based on the above statement, the pavilion must have been attached to the Royal Pharmacy.

> ✿ **Shennong** (神農)： was a legendary ruler of China and culture hero. He is considered to have been one of the Three Emperors who lived some 5,000 years ago. He is thought to have taught the ancient Chinese both their practice of agriculture and the use of herbal drugs.

Passing through the small gate, you will be in the front yard of the Old Seonwonjeon Shrine. Seonwonjeon served as a royal portrait hall in order to worship successive kings. Through demonstrating royal forefather and his descendants, the dynasty intended to ensure royal authority and legitimacy At the portrait hall enshrining portraits of former kings including founder Taejo, the current king would hold rather a simple ancestral rite in person on the first and the fifteenth day every month, and on birthdays and death anniversaries. The Jongmyo (宗廟) Shrine is a national shrine where the spirit tablets of kings and queens were enshrined and grand ceremonies were performed, while Seonwonjeon Shrine is for the royal clan.

Changdeokgung Palace currently has two Seonwonjeon

❖ *Jongmyojerye* (宗廟祭禮) : are ancestral ceremonies held at Jongmyo (Royal Ancestral Shrine) where the spirit tablets of Joseon kings and queens are enshrined. Its main hall enshrines 19 spirit chambers and its annex hall 16 ones. The ceremonies include a regular one, a temporary one, a seasonal one, and a mourning one. They were not strictly performed during the Japanese rule and since 1969 they have been authentically observed on the first Sunday in May every year hosted by Jeonju Lee Royal Family Association. Most of the ceremonies were held by the king, but sometimes by the crown prince or high ranking officials. The procedures are composed of four steps: welcoming ancestors by burning incense and pouring wine to the earth, entertaining ancestors by offering wine three times, getting blessed from the ancestors by sharing the offered wine and food, and then sending off the ancestors.

Shrines: Old and New Seonwonjeon (cf. the 16th chapter of New Seonwonjeon Shrine). In 1921 Japanese authorities removed Daebodan (大報壇) Altar seated at the northwestern section of the palace precincts and built a new building right there, so-called New Seonwonjeon (新璿源展). The old one has remained here as an empty structure. Through Bochunmun Gate in the east you can enter Yangjidang (養志堂) Hall. Yangjidang Hall was the place where the king would stay before the ritual at Seonwonjeon. It was also used to keep the caskets of royal portraits. Record has it that King Yeongjo had his robes kept in the hall.

Yangjidang Hall

Royal Pharmacy (Yakbang)

Leaving Yangjidang, you are heading to the Royal Pharmacy. It is located north of Okdang (玉堂). The pharmacy was responsible for ensuring the health of the king and other royal family members. Chief and vice chief in charge of the pharmacy, accompanied by royal physicians would visit the king, and ask for undergoing a medical checkup every five days.

The Royal Pharmacy presented to the king not only medicine

Royal Pharmacy

Name plaque of Royal Pharmacy

but also tea. They ensured that the tea was prepared using a pot made of silver and water carried from the center of the Han River. To the south of the front yard lies a small gate to the royal nurses' quarters. Royal nurses gave simple medical treatment to female members of the palace.

The pharmacy reminds you of King Yeongjo, a dutiful son. The king repeatedly turned down his medical checkups, which frustrated his court officials. In the 15th year of his reign (1740), King Yeongjo unexpectedly dropped by the tomb of his birth mother on his way back from a visit to Onneung (the tomb of Queen Dangyeong). Queen Dangyeong, the first wife of King Jungjong, was forcefully deposed when the Jungjong Coup (中宗反正) took place in 1506. King Yeongjo restored her queenhood posthumously and paid a visit to her tomb. After returning to the palace the king refused medical exams several times, which perplexed the court officials. The reason was that the officials were inattentive and negligent when they visited his biological mother's grave. He adopted a roundabout expression about his devotion to his mother by alluding to a historical example. Actually he was inwardly expecting his officials to raise his mother's status spontaneously. At the time the main job of the Royal Pharmacy was to keep a close watch on the King's condition and the king's rejection was a matter of serious concern for officials. The incident must have come from King Yeongjo's tactics to materialize his hidden intention by taking advantage of their concern. From the articles dated August 23, 24, 27, and 28, 1740 of King Yeongjo's Annals. "Chief of the Royal Pharmacy Kim Heunggyeong asked the Majesty to have medical exams, which he refused again."

Okdang Hall (Hongmungwan Office)

After looking around the pharmacy and going outside, you will see the Geumcheongyo Bridge and Jinseonmun Gate. Would you take another look over the bridge from its eastern side and go for a visit to Okdang Hall (玉堂: Jade Hall) if you can afford. The hall deserves your attention even if you have some trouble making a detour from the ordinary routine for the tourists. *Okdang* is the nickname of *Hongmungwan* (弘文館: Office of Special

Unconnected inner walls of Okdang

Advisors) and means 'gathering place of people as precious and beautiful as jade.' *Hongmungwan* was the successor of *Jiphyeonjeon* (集賢殿 : Academy of Talented Scholars) and was in charge of research and lecturing. Also, it served as public media in a contemporary sense in that it spared no effort to give frank advice to the king. *Hongmungwan* officials were responsible for maintaining books kept at the palace, making public documents, and attending royal lectures at which the king would read and discuss Confucian classics and history books with his scholar officials. They wrote out the king's commands on paper as the advisory body responding to the king's requests for advice. Along with *Saheonbu* (司憲府 : Office of the Inspector-General) and *Saganwon* (司諫院 : Office of the Censor-General), *Hongmungwan* was called *Samsa* (三司 : the Three Remonstrial Offices) which are the organs responsible for investigating power abuse and representing the views of influential noblemen. Its officials served as attendants to assist the king from close at hand.

Thus the officials of *Hongmungwan* would be descended from prestigious families, secure abilities relevant to their duties, and have enough scholarship and language skills to preside at the royal lectures before the king. They were endowed with status and treatment superior to *Saheonbu* and *Saganwon* officials, in that the king favored *Hongmungwan* officials, presenting them with food and drink, newly published books, and leaves of

74

absence to read books. Everybody regarded *Hongmungwan* officials with envy, calling their positions '*clean and important positions* (清要職).' That is because becoming *Hongmungwan* officials meant they gained in officialdom their footings by which they could be promoted to more high-ranking offices.

Okdang was readily accessible to the king and quite essential in the Gwolnaegaksa compound. It seems the king dealt with political affairs by visiting the hall frequently. Since one of its functions was to maintain books, Nusanggo (樓上庫) Storage and Deungyeongnu (登瀛樓) Pavilion attached with a narrow staircase in the eastern section of Okdang seem to have stored book-related materials.

In the yard of Okdang stand some unconnected inner walls. Even though the Okdang yard is not large, a couple of inner walls are erected to shield the hall from the outer quarters that were

Maehwa is in blossom after a long winter

vulnerable to exposure. Partitioning seems to have intended to visually add a sense of stability and to inform people that the hall was an important facility the king often called at. You see a *maehwa* tree inside the inner wall. When spring comes, the small yard of Okdang is fragrant with *maehwa* blossoms as precious as jade.

75

4

Injeongjeon Hall
Practicing Benevolent Governance

Government Offices Inside the Palace were also located
in the front yard outside Injeongmun Gate
to carry out important events.

After you cross Geumcheongyo Bridge, you will face the second gate, Jinseonmun (進善門) Gate. During the reigns of King Taejong and King Yeongjo, a drum called *sinmungo* or *deungmungo* was installed at the gate to receive civil complaints or petitions. As a matter of fact, though, it must have been unimaginable for commoners to get enter the strictly forbidden palace in the first place, passing through such a big gate, and

Geumcheongyo Bridge and Jinseonmun Gate

beat the drum to file a civil complaint. The fact that they installed *sinmungo* or *deungmungo* as was written in the *Annals of the Joseon Dynasty* shows that Joseon kings at least tried to communicate with the people even though it ended up being only a formal gesture.

The system was abolished and resumed off and on due to the confusion caused by frequent false accusations. However, we can also know that the system was actually practiced from an article of the *Annals of King Taejong* (January 26, 1402, the second year of King Taejong). It says that King Taejong ordered *Euijeongbu* (the State Council) to let the civil petitioner who suffered any undeserved thing beat the drum first, and ask his or her identity and address later.

Passing through Jinseonmun Gate, you will find another courtyard spreading around the long three-lane road in front of Injeongmun Gate. The fact that other Government Offices Inside the Palace were located in that yard lets us imagine the scale of the important ceremonies held in the Injeongjeon area.

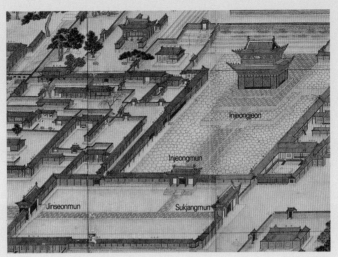
Injeongjeon area in the *Painting of the Eastern Palaces*

❖ *Gwollaegaksa* (Government Offices Inside the Palace) in front of Injeongmun Gate

Jeongcheong (Office in charge of personnel affairs related with Ministry of Personnel and Ministry of Military Affairs)

Naebyeongjo (Court Office in charge of military affairs and facilities)

Howicheong (Office in charge of attending on the king and escorting him)

Sangseowon (Office in charge of handling royal seals, tokens of king's authorization for an official's requisition of horses on his regional trip, certificates of appointment, etc)

It gives us a special sentiment to see Injeongjeon Hall
that remains undaunted by numerous historical ordeals.

Passing through the Injeongmun (仁政門) Gate, at the end of the three-lane road, you come to face Injeongjeon (仁政殿) Hall standing on the high stone platform, or *woldae*. The *ilwoldam* (the wall inlaid with sun and moon shaped bricks) spreading at the back of Injeongjeon seems to embrace the harmony between *yin* and *yang* of the universe as the term '*ilwol* (日月: the sun and the moon)'

Injeongmun Gate

East corridor building of the Injeongjeon Hall compound

referring to the wall literally stands for yin and yang. The corridor buildings to the east and the west of Injeongjeon look commanding like wings widely outstretched. Seen from outside Injeongmun Gate, Injeongjeon still looks imposing, undaunted despite various historical ordeals that it went through.

Let's now take a look at the spacious yard before the Injeongmun Gate. In this yard, very important state events were held. Among them was an audience called *jocham* when all the civil and the military officials greeted the king in the morning. According to *Gyeongguk daejeon*(The Grand Code for State Administration), it was held on the fifth, eleventh, 21st, and 25th day of each month. Enthronement ceremonies were also held right in the yard in front of the Injeongmun Gate. After the king passed away, the crown prince dressed in mourning attire on the sixth day of the state mourning period, which qualified him as the successor to the throne, and he was granted the *daebo* (the Royal Seal). Then he had the enthronement ceremony by being seated on the temporary throne laid at the center of the place in front of the Injeongmun Gate. Most of the crown princes were enthroned at the gate of the main throne hall of the palace. It is presumable that, with the status of crown prince, he could not be seated on the formal throne inside the main throne hall until after he became king. Eight Joseon kings were enthroned at the Injeongmun Gate of Changdeokgung Palace: Yeonsangun, Hyojong, Hyeonjeong, Sukjong, Yeongjo, Sunjo, Cheoljong, and Gojong.

Injeongjeon Hall seen from the southeast corridor

A Tearful Enthronement Ceremony

Most of the enthronement ceremonies of the kings were performed during the state funeral of the previous king with everyone grieving except when the throne was abdicated in favor of the next king (while the former king was still alive) or usurped by a coup. Therefore, the commonly produced scenes of a splendid, magnificent, and happy enthronement in many historical TV dramas or movies are not based upon correct research and lead the viewers to be unconsciously mistaken.

When the king passed away, the first thing they did was to establish *Binjeondogam* (Office of the Royal Coffin Hall), an ad hoc committee. They chose the Royal Coffin Hall from among the palace buildings where they would lay the coffin of the deceased king in state. The crown prince who would succeed the throne stayed in the mourning hut temporarily installed near the Royal Coffin Hall. On the sixth day after the former king's decease, he put on mourning attire, and on the same day the enthronement was solemnly carried out.

The enthronement ceremony consisted of two major parts. The testament containing the deceased king's will was delivered

The front yard of Injeongmun Gate where the enthronement ceremony was held.

to the succeeding king from the prime minister in the Royal
Coffin Hall. Then he was granted the king's royal seal by the first
vice-premier. Next, he was seated on the throne which was
installed in the center of the gate of the main throne hall
compound facing south, and accepted felicitations from the
officials. The attire the new king was wearing at the
enthronement was not a mourning garment, but the formal

ceremonial robe with a nine-symbol design and the royal crown with nine strings of beads while the officials wore the gold cap and the court attire. After the ceremony was over, the king and the officials changed into mourning attire again.

To take an example from King Sukjong's enthronement ceremony, when the previous king Heonjong passed away, Seonjeongjeon Hall was designated as the Royal Coffin Hall. For a few days, the crown prince kept refusing to accede to the throne, saying that he just could not do so. However, on the sixth day, he changed into mourning attire in the mourning hut as scheduled, and finally accepted the royal seal in the Royal Coffin Hall in a kneeling position wearing the formal ceremonial robe and the royal crown. After he finished the ritual of incense burning, the crown prince passed through Yeonyeongmun Gate, Sukjangmun Gate, and reached the venue for the enthronement ceremony in front of the Injeongmun Gate. Here he did again decline several times in tears to ascend to the throne. However, after the repeated earnest imploration of the ministers, he finally ascended to the throne and accepted congratulations from the subjects. All the government officials bowed down four times, and cheered "A thousand years, a thousand years, and thousands of thousand years!"

Although the royal court orchestra was prepared, they did not play music. After the enthronement ceremony, the king ascended to Injeongjeon Hall stepping on the king's lane, and then went back to the mourning hut. There he changed into his mourning attire again, and continued to play the role of the chief mourner. Like this, even though ascending to the throne was a tremendously significant state affair, the atmosphere was extremely somber and sorrowful as it was held during the mourning period of the late king.

When all the procedures were completed, the official message of the enthronement was promulgated by the official who was in charge of reading state messages. The Royal Secretariat forwarded the official documents to each provincial governing authority to inform of the enthronement of the new king nationwide.

King's Main Throne Hall, Injeongjeon Hall

Now you are in the Injeongjeon Hall compound. Why do you not think about the meaning of the name 'Injeongjeon?' It can be interpreted as 'Hall of Benevolent Governance' since 'injeong (仁政)' refers to 'benevolent ruling.' It originated from the government ruled by a virtuous king emphasized by Mencius.

As the main throne hall in Changdeokgung, the Injeongjeon Hall compound was a venue for various state official ceremonies such as the king's enthronement, the crown prince's investiture, weddings, audiences, receptions for foreign envoys, and national examinations for recruiting officials. Injeongjeon Hall is a 5-kan-long and 4-kan wide building with double hip-and-gable styled roofs. It is a single-story structure with the interior open to the high ceiling even though it looks like a two-story building when seen from the outside. The size, height, and decoration of Injeongjeon including the high stone platform or *woldae*, and the roof figurines called *japsang* are all commensurate with the significance of the building and the authority of the king.

The stone terraces at the back of Injeongjeon Hall were set up to relay the vital energy from the Baekdu-daegan Mountain

The *oyat* flower pattern as the imperial coat of arms on the main ridge of the roof of Injeongjeon

System which flows along Mt. Bukan, Bohyeonbong Peak, Mt. Bugak, and Eungbong Peak in turn. The rear wall is called *ilwoldam*, which means a wall embedded with round designs symbolizing the protection of the sun, the moon, and the stars. The simple round and parallel designs of the bricks along the long wall are not as splendid as those of other flower-patterned brick walls, but harmonious and graceful enough.

There are five ✿*oyat* flower patterns made by casting copper on the roof ridge of Injeongjeon. People call it *ihwa munjang* (*oyat* flower as the imperial coat of arms) symbolizing the Joseon Dynasty (including The Great Han Empire). The scientific name of *oyat* is as same as that of plum, but *oyat* is a kind of plum indigenous to Korea. There are three oyat flower patterns on both sides of the roof ridge of Injeongmun gate. However, on the roof ridge of Injeongjeon Hall, only five *oyat* flower patterns on the front side still remain, with the back side ones all missing.

After Emperor Gojong abdicated his throne in favor of his son Sunjong, Emperor Sunjong moved into Changdeokgung Palace. Based upon the first article of October 7th, 1907 of the *Annals of Emperor Sunjong*, it can be presumed that the *oyat* flower

✿ **The *oyat* flower pattern** : Better known as '*ihwa*', it is a plum flower pattern, used as the imperial coat of arms of the Great Han Empire. Even though it is also found to have been used in the decoration of palaces and in the designs of some currencies at the end of the Joseon period, it began to be used as the official imperial coat of arms of the Great Han Empire. The design was used not only in architecture such as Injeongjeon at Changeokgung and Seokjojeon Hall at Deoksugung but also in medals, military uniforms, and craftwork for the imperial family. The design is made by patterning the *oyat* flower in a simplified form and arranging five petals in a left-right symmetrical array with three pistils. Some other imperial family members modified the basic pattern and made their own emblems. For example, the Unhyeongung family surrounded the petals with a circle, and the Sadonggung family used the pattern with its petals surrounded by two concentric circles. Only the imperial family and the members of the Great Han Empire could use the *oyat* flower patterns, and they were widely used in their living space and for their household items.

patterns might have been added to the roof ridge of Injeongjeon during the renovation of Changdeokgung before Emperor Sunjong moved into the palace.

Seen from the picture inserted in the Illustrated Record of Korean Historical Sites, which was compiled by the Japanese Government General authorities, Injeongjeon Hall did not have

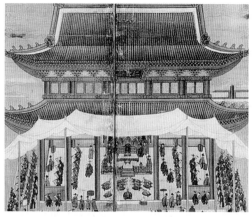

A Part of the *Injeongjeon Jinhado* (Painting on the celebration of Queen Dowager Sunwon's sixtieth birthday, and Queen Dowager Sinjeong of forty-first birthday at Injeongjeon Hall)

the *oyat* flower patterns at that time. The picture was taken by a Japanese researcher of architecture history, Sekino Tadashi (1867~1935), when he investigated old historical buildings remaining in Joseon from 1902 to 1904. The *oyat* flower pattern is quite Japanesy, and had not been used for traditional Joseon architecture. It is not certain whether the introduction of the pattern was from the Great Han Empire's own decision or by the influence of Japan, considering the circumstances of the period.

However, considering the atmosphere from the end of the 19th century to the beginning of the 20th century, it is noteworthy that Emperor Gojong was very open and active in adopting Western culture. The Great Han Empire was founded by Emperor Gojong in 1897 after Japan defeated Qing China in the

94

first Sino-Japanese war in 1895. Then Emperor Gojong needed to make a new national flag and imperial coat of arms. During the period, the patterns were used not only for medals, and military uniforms but also for all imperial property, including coins. Pottery and stamps also had the *oyat* flower designs. By that time, Seokjojeon Hall in Deoksugung Palace also already had the design. Therefore, when Emperor Sunjong renovated Changdeokgung Palace into a Western style, where he was going to move into, he might have already accepted the mounting of the *oyat* flower design onto the main roof ridge of Injeongjeon Hall without any repulsion. Despite the negative dubious that the design might have been granted by the Japanese emperor to the diminished royal Yi clan, just as a family coat of arms, when the Great Han Empire had almost lost its sovereignty, the *oyat* flower pattern still should be considered as the official imperial coat of arms of the Great Han Empire.

The *ilwoldam* wall inlaid with the bricks symbolizing
the sun and the moon

The Courtyard and *Bakseok*

Beyond the threshold of Injeongmun Gate, the quite solemn space of the king unfolds. The clean-cut square courtyard was called jojeong.

The yard is paved with pieces of roughly hewn granite slabstone called *bakseok*. Paving the courtyard with *bakseok* meant Injeongjeon compound was an important space for major ceremonies. Practically, *bakseok* prevents the yard from getting muddy from the rainwater, but, it is all the more significant in that it gives a visually solemn effect.

The courtyard of Injeongjeon Hall paved with *bakseok*

Bakseok is not smoothly hewn stone. Instead of polishing the surface, they rather fully brought life to the rough texture of granite stone. The stone was cut thinly along the grain to the thickness of 10 to 20 centimeters. Each piece of the stone may look rough, nevertheless, the effect made by covering the whole courtyard with such crude stone slabs is uncomparably more high-spirited and graver than the mechanical touch of neatly smoothed stones. Such a difference certainly reveals itself when we compare the texture of the old *bakseok* used in some parts of the west yard near the southern corridor and the stone platform of Injeongjeon Hall with that of the newly restored *bakseok* in the rest of the area.

According to some records, *bakseok* used in the Joseon palaces were mainly supplied from Haeju of Hwanghaedo Province and Ganghwado Island. During the Japanese occupation period, they destroyed *bakseok* in the courtyard of Injeongjeon to lay grass instead. It is extremely regrettable that we recently restored the courtyard of Injeongjeon with granite stones which were mechanically cut and artificially dented. I am lost for words to express regret about such insensibility as dinting the stone with a machine. Nevertheless, despite all, the grandeur of Injeongjeon Hall standing high against the backdrop of *ilwoldam* wall is still unflinching, and seems to tell it is the very seat of the mighty monarch.

Three-lane Road and Rank Stones

Entering Injeongmun Gate, we can see that the three-lane road which started from Geumcheongyo Bridge continues all the way through Jinseonmun Gate and up to the stone platform of Injeongjeon Hall. Among the three lanes, the middle lane is wider and slightly higher than the others. As was custom, Matter-of-coursely, it was the king's lane while the east lane was for civil officials and the west for military officials. The word

Three-lane road and rank stones

An iron ring to fix the marquee

'*yangban* (兩班: both branches)' commonly referring to the noble class originated from the same word literally meaning both branches of administration called *munban* (civil officials or east branch) and *muban* (military officials or west branch).

Two arrays of rank stones to the left and to the right of the three-lane road were installed during the reign of King Jeongjo to straighten the disrupted order of ✿ranks in the government by marking the grades of the officials. It can be regarded as King Jeongjo's groundwork signaling his strong volition to innovate the court and restore the weakened kingship.

By the way, can you see there are unexpected things sticking out on the courtyard? Big iron rings are stuck in the granite slabs near the rank stones for the senior third degree officials. Out of curiosity, one may feel tempted to hold it up to figure out what the thing was for, only to find it quite heavy. Those rings were used to fix the marquee for national ceremonies held in the courtyard. They are found on the stone platforms of Injeongjeon, and also on the outer horizontal beams and pillars of the hall.

✿ **Rank system of the government officials during the Joseon Dynasty :** Grades of Joseon officials consisted of nine ranks from the first to the ninth degree. Each rank was divided into *jeong* and *jong* (like senior and junior), and the posts above the junior sixth degree were subdivided into *sanggye* and *hagye* (like upper class and lower class), making the total to 30 classes. In the courtyard, two lines of twelve rank stones are set up, one line to the east and the other to the west. From the first to the third rank, there are separate rank stones for the senior and the junior degrees, however, from the forth to the ninth ranks, there are rank stones only for the senior degree officials. High ranking officials of upper senior third or higher degrees were collectively called '*dangsanggwan* (palace-ascendable officials),' while officials from the lower senior third degree to the junior sixth degree were called '*danghagwan* (palace-downward officials)' or '*chamsang*,' and officials below the senior seventh degree were differentiated being called '*chamha*.' '*Dangsanggwan*' literally means the ministers and high ranking officials who were authorized to ascend to the hall to participate in discussions of state affairs with the king.

However, the marquee rings are not stuck all around the courtyard. Here is the very reality of the hierarchical Joseon society. As the marquee was set up only for the king, the ministers, and officials of senior third and higher degrees, the rest of the officials could not but wait till the event was over, patiently enduring the hot sunshine. Moreover, they did not dare to get into trouble by loosening their posture no matter how hard it might be to withstand the sunlight, as they were quite well aware that they were being watched by the hawk-eyed inspectors of the Office of Inspector General.

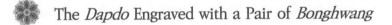

The *Dapdo* Engraved with a Pair of *Bonghwang*

The three-lane road leads to the steps of the *woldae*. The king's lane is connected to the royal staircase with a slanted stone engraved with a pair of birds. The stone is called *dapdo*, which literally means 'stepping stone.' However, the stone was rather a symbol of the royal path as the king actually did not step on the stone, but was carried in a sedan chair.

Though weathered by wind and rain for a long time, on the *dapdo* is a relief of two imaginary birds called *bonghwang*. According to the legend, *bonghwang* is a pair of birds (also known

The three-lane road leads to the steps of the *woldae*.

as Chinese phoenix, fenghuang) which were thought to be as numinous as a dragon, a qilin, and a turtle, collectively called the 'four benevolent animals.' The male bird called bong and the female bird called *hwang* always appear together as a pair. They never eat a live animal, neither break a branch of a live plant or a tree, nor can be enmeshed in nets. They neither flock together, nor eat anything but clean dewdrops and bamboo fruit. They appear only when the whole country is peaceful and prosperous.

They disappear when a monarch misrules the country, people fall into poverty, or when the country becomes turbulent. I wonder whether such a peaceful and prosperous era has ever existed in human history; or, have all the kings ever been conscious of the legend of *bonghwang*, considering that common people have always been in poverty as well as suppressed and overwhelmed by the authority of the dominant class. The rulers must have at least felt obliged to usher in a peaceful and prosperous era regardless of the result.

Carried over the *dapdo* engraved with *bonghwang* idly flying in clouds, and finally being seated on the throne, the king stood out as a holy being who could spread a moral and edifying ruling as a sage monarch. *Bonghwang* was a metaphor of the wish of the people who longed for the appearance of a sage king.

dapdo

104

The central staircase leading to Injeongjeon Hall

The cloud design on the handrail of a staircase leading to Injeongjeon

The Interior of Injeongjeon Hall
Remodeled in a Western Style

At last, let's take a look at the inside of Injeongjeon Hall. When Emperor Sunjong moved into Changdeokgung Palace, Western-style furniture and interior decoration were introduced. The remodeled structure shows various differences from the traditional style. The black bricks on the floor were removed and Western style parquet flooring was laid. Electric lamps were also installed. The fire-proof brick window base were replaced with big panels of wooden window bases. The doors were remodeled

The interior of Injeongjeon Hall

Western-style curtains in Injeongjeon Hall

to be opened from the inside, and the inner glass windows were added to the existing windows. Curtain boxes were also made to hang curtains and drapes.

Would you raise your head and look up at the ceiling? Seen from outside, Injeongjeon seemed to be a two-story building, but it is actually a single-story structure with the interior open to the high ceiling. The multi-colored painting called dancheong on the ceiling is very brilliant with lotus flower and *bonghwang* patterns. Buildings with multi brackets between two pillars usually have a coffered ceiling, which is inserted with square panel coffers and painted with *dancheong*. Such a style of ceiling is called a checkered ceiling. In Injeongjeon, the center part of the

The throne in the center of Injeongjeon is elaborately adorned.

checkered ceiling is raised a little bit to make a recess. It is decorated with many layers of small colorful ancones to make a canopy ceiling. The canopy ceiling is presumed to have been modeled after an umbrella unfolded for a noble man. On the middle of the canopy ceiling, a pair of *bonghwang* as a symbol of the king's sovereignty are hanging tightly to small iron rings like a mobile.

The throne is lacated in the north center of Injeongjeon hall. It is elevated very high, and its back and the armrests are elaborately adorned in an openwork technique. The patterns are mostly of dragons, and lotus and peony flowers. The three-folded wooden screen behind the throne is also decorated mainly with dragons, lotuses, and peonies.

Ilwolobongbyeong Screen is placed behind the three-folded wooden screen. The picture on the screen is called *Ilwolobongdo* Painting or ✿ *Ilwoloakdo* Painting. Against the backdrop of the blue sky, the red sun in the east and the white moon in the west are shining over five mountain peaks. There are two pine trees with red trunks, cascades of mightily falling water from both valleys are raising clouds of spray, and the rolling waves are

✿ *Ilwoloakdo* : The nature depicted in *Ilwolobongdo* Painting is interpreted as expressing the content of a poem 'Cheonbo' in Chinese *Shijing* (詩經: the Book of Poetry). It symbolizes royal sovereignty as endowed by heaven, the eternal succession of the dynasty as well as the Neo-Confucian ruling ideology. The painting solemnly supports the authority of the king.

The throne decorated with patterns of dragon and peony

spreading below the mountains. '*Ilwol*' stands for 'the sun and the moon,' of which meaning can be stretched to the concept of the universe that the king takes control of five peaks refer to the whole territory where the king's sovereignty reaches over as Mt. Gollyun (a legendary mountain in China) does. In the Korean Peninsula, the five peaks are Mt. Baekdu in the north, Mt. Jiri in the south, Mt. Geumgang in the east, Mt. Myohyang in the west, and Mt. Bukhan in the center. The waves in the painting meant the royal court where the king conducted the state affairs. The symbol was derived from the coincidence of the pronunciations of the letter *jo* (潮: waves) and of *jo* (朝: the first letter of jojeong which means royal court).

Above the throne of Injeongjeon, you will find a structure similar to that placed over the statue of Buddha in temples. The structure is a wooden canopy, which is installed to emphasize the dignity of royal authority. It is brilliantly decorated with multi-layered brackets. Under the brackets are hidden symbols hung to ward off fires. They are short mock poles of which the ends are carved into lotus buds. The lotus buds submerged in water symbolize that the building itself is already deep in water so that it will not be burnt by fire. Although we cannot see it from outside, another pair of bonghwang is also hanging on the inner ceiling of the canopy.

The engravings on the sides of the stairs where the throne is laid in Injeongjeon

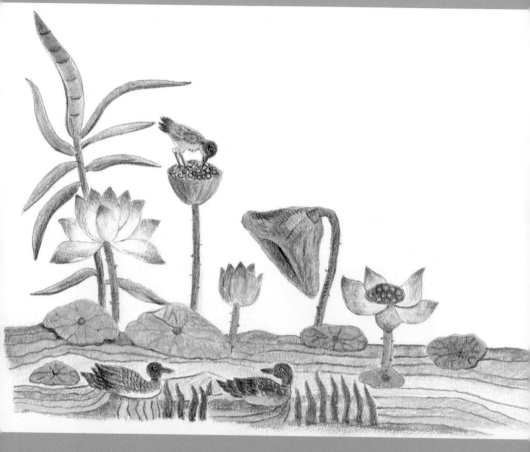

Painting with the same theme of the engravings on the sides of
the stairs where the throne is laid in Injeongjeon

Roof Figurines, *Japsang*

The roof figurines of Injeongjeon

Now let's turn our eyes to the outside and take a look at the small figurines on the protruding corners of the hip of the roof. Those figurines called *japsang*, (which literally means sundry figurines) are a kind of decorative tiles only used for palace buildings. They were fixed on the roof to watch the sky and guard the royal palace from evil spirits coming from the air. In Korea, there are ten kinds of *japsang*. They are characters in the novel *Journey to the West* and the other deities of the earth. The first majestic one is the Buddhist priest of Tang China, Xuanzang. The next ones are the disciples like Monkey King, Pig Monster, and Half Water Demon in order. They are placed on the roofs of the palaces as the strongest group in the novel that defeated all the evil spirits of the world on their journey to India, searching for Buddhist Scriptures to bring them to Tang China. *Japsang* in Korean palaces have additional meanings for warding off evil spirits while the Chinese counterparts consist of a Taoistic hermit riding a Chinese phoenix and other auspicious animals like a dragon, fenghuang, mythical lion, and a seahorse. It may seem contradictory that the Joseon Dynasty, founded upon the ruling ideology of Confucianism, let the Buddhist figurines guard the palaces. The original Taoistic figurines like those in China might have been used during the earlier period of Joseon, but Buddhist figurines must have replaced the original ones when *Journey to the West* was translated during the reign of King Seonjo, and gained popularity as they could ward off evil spirits.

The rest of the figurines among the *japsang* are not always mounted by rule. Sometimes, the same ones were even repeated.

In Korea, the number of the roof figurines does not necessarily match with the importance of the buildings while in China, the higher number of roof figurines was set on the more important buildings. However, put mostly in odd numbers, the number naturally tends to match roughly with the scale of the buildings.

The handle of *deumeu*

The big water pot on the corner of the stone platform *woldae* is called '*deumeu.*' It is movable with handles. It was a kind of fire-fighting equipment filled with water in case of a fire. The traditional Joseon architecture mostly made of wood was vulnerable to fires except for the roof tiles, foundation stones and the stone walls. Moreover, the palace structures built with narrow walls in between and connected with one another by corridors or corridor buildings were even more prone to fires.

Deumeu on the corner of the *woldae*

The Joseon people believed that fire monsters came from heaven. They wished that the monster approaching the building would get scared by its own horrible reflection on the water in *deumeu*, and instantly fly away. Even though *deumeu* could practically be used to put out fire, it had more meaning in driving out evil spirits.

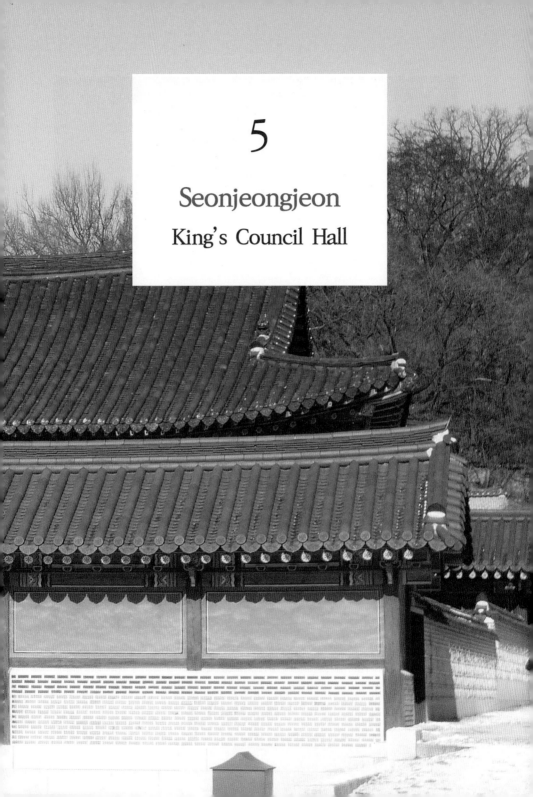

5

Seonjeongjeon
King's Council Hall

The view from *cheollang* corridor penetrating into the center
of the Seonjeongjeon compound.

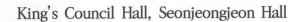

King's Council Hall, Seonjeongjeon Hall

Outside the Gwangbeommun Gate in the east of Injeongjeon Hall, a spacious yard stretches out, and to the north of the yard, Seonjeongjeon (宣政殿) Hall, the king's council hall of Changdeokgung is located. 'Sejonjeong (宣政)' means 'to spread governance and edification widely.' In Seonjeongjeon, a daily morning audience with the king called *sangcham* was held, when the ministers, senior retainers, palace-ascendable high ranking officials of

King's throne in Seonjeongjeon

119

major public offices, royal lecturers, a secretary, and the chroniclers attended regularly to report and discuss the state affairs. During King Myeongjong's reign, his mother, the Queen Dowager Munjeong ruled the country from behind the bamboo screen in Seonjeongjeon Hall.

Bonghwang on the ceiling of the canopy above the throne

Between Seonjeongjeon Hall and Seonjeongmun Gate, there is an open-sided corridor with a roof, and it juts into the middle of the compound. This type of corridor is called a *cheollang*. Unlike most buildings which had corridors surrounding the compound, the Seonjeongjeon compound has a *cheollang*, which is evidence that Seonjeongjeon was also used as a ✿Royal Spirit Tablet Hall.

✿ **Royal Spirit Tablet Hall** : While the building that the king or the queen's coffin was placed for five months in the palace was called the Royal Coffin Hall, the one enshrining their spirit tablet in the palace after the coffin was buried in the royal tomb was called the Royal Spirit Tablet Hall. After the state mourning period for three years (actually 26 months after the death) was over, the king's spirit table was enshrined in the national shrine *Jongmyo*. However, if the queen passed away earlier than the king, her spirit tablet was kept in the Royal Spirit Tablet Hall until it could be enshrined later in Jongmyo with that of the king.

Seonjeongjeon, the only Building with Blue-glazed Roof tiles

Among the Joseon palace buildings, Seonjeongjeon is the only remaining one with blue-glazed roof tiles. The roof reveals its splendor when it is seen from a distance. Blue-glazed roof tiles were used instead of conventional charcoal gray ones when the king wanted to build an imposing edifice in the palaces.

According to the *Diary of Gwanghaegun*, in the *Annals of the*

Seonjeongjeon Hall

Joseon Dynasty, there are many articles describing the scenes of the *Yeonggeondogam*, the ad-hoc committee of palace construction, requesting the purchase of an ingredient to make blue-glazed roof tiles. Unlike ordinary charcoal gray ones, they required high fuel cost and labor cost since they needed a glazed firing. Naturally, many officials objected to using such luxurious blue-glazed roof tiles. In the Diary, however, we can see King Gwanghaegun, who later was dethroned, permitting the purchase of niter, an ingredient for making the glaze.

At the end of the third article written on the 27th day of June in 1717 (the ninth year of King Gwanghaegun), the chronicler added his comment, as follows.

The chronicler comments, "The great ancient Chinese emperors Yao and Shun are unexceptionally referred to when we mention benevolent ruling even though they lived in a very humble thatched-roof house built only on a three-tiered earth foundation. At the end of the Xia Dynasty, a benevolent emperor said Kunwu was luxurious since he used roof tiles. Nevertheless, how can we now think that we can make Seoul stand out only by glaze firing the roof tiles of the throne hall with extremely expensive grayish blue pigment *hoehoecheong?* It has to be imported from tens of thousand kilometers away, especially during this hard period, when the nation is facing difficulties due to carrying out an unnecessarily grand-scale palace construction. I deeply feel regretful that the officials in charge of the ad-hoc committee still insist on doing every thing in such a luxurious and excessive manner despite the difficulties, not even one person appealing and trying at all to correct the negative consequences of such custom."

As for the above mentioned article, the chronicler must have mistaken *hoehoecheong* (the imported grayish blue pigment for making pocelain jars) for niter (an expensive ingredient of gunpowder for making blue-glazed roof tiles). *Hoehoecheong* that the chronicler mentioned was actually a pigment used for making blue-and-white porcelain jars (*cheonghwa baekja*). Actually, no article is found recording the purchase of the grayish blue pigment *hoehoecheong* in the *Dairy of Gwanghaegun*. Instead, articles are frequently found pushing the purchase of niter to be used as a fusing agent helping color formation of blue-glazed roof tiles. On the other hand, *hoehoecheong* used for making blue-and-white porcelain jars was a kind of cobalt, which was extremely expensive and rare, being imported from Arabia, and the cost was as much as that of gold. During the earlier period of Joseon, even the court painters of *Dohwaseo* (the Royal Bureau of Painting) went to the government kilns in Gwangju in person to paint the drawings on the porcelain not to waste the expensive *hoehoecheong* pigment.

However, since the Japanese invasions of 1592 to 1598, due

to the financial difficulties of the government, tireless effort was made to develop domestic grayish blue pigments. Instead of using the expensive *hoehoecheong*, porcelain jars with underglaze-iron became popular. By the end of the Joseon Dynasty, as the price of iron-brown pigments got affordable, numerous porcelain jars with underglaze-iron were produced. In conclusion, the article shows how the chronicler under the next monarch was subjectively and proudly judging the dethroned king Gwanghaegun, not to mention his misunderstanding about the material used for making blue-glazed roof tiles. Yet in reality, history is always bound to be recorded by the winners.

The Site of Government Offices Inside the Palace in the Front Yard of Seonjeongjeon

On the spacious yard in front of Seonjeongmun Gate, a dashing pine tree and a multi-stemmed pine tree are growing currently, and the cafe in the opposite side seems to have a quite classical grace. Actually, the yard was formerly the site where the eastern Government Offices Inside the Palace were located.

It would be quite enticing to find the locations of now-gone

The front yard of Seonjeongmun Gate

Daecheong, *Seungjeongwon*, and *Saongwon* in the *Painting of the Eastern Palaces*.

Seungjeongwon was the Royal Secretariat where the secretaries in charge of passing out the king's orders worked. All the state affairs were reported to the king in a written document, and were transmitted to the subjects. Being in charge of receiving and passing out those documents meant they had a grip on the overall information of the whole government. Considering that the royal secretaries had to wait on the king day and night, it was natural that *Seungjeongwon* was located at the closest place to the king's council hall, Seonjeongjeon.

Seonjeongjeon area in the *Painting of the Eastern Palaces*

Naebanwon was the Office of Eunuchs. They were in charge of the access roster, transmitting king's orders, inspecting royal meals, guarding the gates, cleaning, and the other sundry duties in the palace.

Saongwon was not only in charge of procuring food for the

126

royal family members but also supplying the food vessels. *Saongwon* operated kilns producing ceramics for the royal court of the Joseon Dynasty. ✿The regional government kilns were called as *Bunwon*. Gwangju *Bunwon* in Gyeonggido Province was the main regional kiln that provided ceramics for the royal court. The best potters made the ceramics of such high quality in Gwangju *Bunwon* that even the Chinese Imperial Court requested Joseon to provide them with their products.

There is a cafe named 'Donggwolmaru' facing Seonjeongjeon. Here once stood a royal garage called *Eochago* where the Emperor Sunjong's and the Empress Sunjeonghyo's vehicles were exhibited from the Japanese occupation period until 2010.

✿ **Installation of regional government kilns of *Saongwon*** : For the earlier period of Joseon, the royal court imposed on some local governments tributes of white porcelains as well as buncheong ware, grayish-blue-powdered celadons produced in regions like Gwangju, Goryeong, and Namwon. Among them, the porcelains were needed more and more as they were widely used not only for the royal court events and royal gifts but also for serving foreign envoys. As the demand grew, the royal court installed regional government kilns to meet the demand of the large amount of fine quality porcelains, instead of depending on the tributes. Regional government kilns of *Saongwon* were installed in Gwangju, which had been providing fine quality porcelains. It is believed that Gwangju *Bunwon* was installed and operated from around 1467.

On the site where *Bincheong* used to be, *Eochago*, the Royal Garage, was once built, and now it has been changed to a cafe named 'Donggwolmaru.'

However, the site was where *Bincheong* (a conference room for the high ranking government officials) was originally located. the *Bincheong* was a conference room for the high ranking officials of *Bibyeonsa*, the Border Defense Council of Joseon, including the prime minister, vice premiers, ministers, and the other palace-ascendable officials who stayed and discussed the pending issues before and after the cabinet meeting in the king's presence. As its status was high among the Government Offices Inside the Palace, it is depicted as an independent compound surrounded with walls in the *Painting of the Eastern Palaces*.

There was another conference room called *Daecheong* in the southern part of the western corridor building of the Seonjeongjeon compound, at the outer area of Sukjangmun Gate. In *Daecheong*, supervising councillors stood by consulting with each other. According to *Hangyeongjiryak* (a history book of old Seoul during the Joseon Dynasty), *Daecheong* is introduced like this.

"*Daecheong* is a conference room where the officials of the Office of the Inspector-General and the Office of the Censor-General waited when they wanted to admonish the king of his obligations. There had been a room installed with an *ondol* heating system in *Daecheong*. During King Sukjong's reign, the officials revered the custom of remonstrating so much and they never stopped admonishing the king even on a cold day that the king should not turn a deaf ear to them, and finally the enraged king got rid of the heated room. From that time on, *Daecheong* did not have heated rooms but a wooden floor hall."

During the Joseon Dynasty, there were very influential Three Remonstration Offices called the *Saheonbu* (Office of Inspector General), *Saganwon* (Office of Censor) and *Hongmungwan* (Office of

Royal Advisors). Not only high ranking officials but also the king himself could not ignore what they said. They gathered in *Daecheong* day and night continuing arguing pros and cons, and they were so proud and high in spirits that King Sukjong came to detest them, and finally removed the *ondol* heated room from the building. Later, the meaning of the word *Daecheong* was changed to mean a wooden-floored hall without a heating system. How bitingly cold the officials must have felt sitting on the *daecheong* floor in midwinter! Nevertheless, such a drastic measure taken by King Sukjong does not seem to have succeeded in clipping their wings.

Bogyeongdang Hall and *Janggo* on the Way to Huijeongdang Hall

On the way to Huijeongdang Hall from Seonjeongjeon is a quite spacious empty yard to the north. Now there are only some weedy stone terraced tiers. However, there had been many buildings on the site. According to the *Painting of the Eastern Palaces*, the stone terraced tiers were *Janggo* which the Royal Kitchen took care of, where jars of sauces and condiments were placed. From the west to the east on the yard were Bogyeongdang, Taehwadang, and Jaedeokdang Halls side by side. Hush! Something around here seems to tell us that this space must have a special story. How about stopping for a moment, and listening attentively to the story?

Bogyeongdang (寶慶堂) Hall was the living quarters of Lady Sukbin Choi who was a concubine of King Sukjong, and the birthplace of King Yeongjo. She gave a birth to the prince in Bogyeongdang in September of 1694 (the 20th year of King Sukjong). The prince Yeoninggun later became King Yeongjo succeeding to the throne after King Gyeongjong. After he had a wedding ceremony, he moved out of the palace, and lived in Changuigung Palace (located to the southwest of Gyeongbokgung Palace).

The site where *Janggo* and Bogyeongdang were located

When King Yeongjo was a prince, he asked his mother, who was from a low social status, what the hardest thing was when she was a court attendant. On hearing her answer that quilting was the most arduous job, it is said that he threw away his quilted arm warmers right away, and never wore quilted clothes for the rest of his life from then on.

Judging from this story, we may think that Lady Sukbin Choi might not have been a *musuri*, the court attendant of the lowest status.

Considering the time when she first met King Sukjong, she might have been assigned to a needlework room after Queen Inhyeon was demoted to an ordinary person and expelled to her private home. Prince Yeoninggun, the son of Lady Sukbin Choi, obtained investiture as the crown prince since he was the step brother of King Gyeongjong, and finally was enthroned in August of 1724. He become the 21st king of the Joseon Dynasty, Yeongjo. He dropped by Bogyeongdang frequently, and left the following reminiscent essay, '*Bogyeongdang gihoe.*' The essay full of his filial piety and longing for his mother is included in *Gunggwolji* (Book of Palaces).

"Oh! There is Bogyeongdang lying west of Daejojeon Hall in Changdeokgung. It is the very place where I was born. Oh! My mother gave birth to me on September 13 in the 20th year of the late father of mine, King Sukjong. When I was nineteen, I moved out to a private home, but whenever I visited the Palace, I stayed in this hall with mother. When I was thirty-one, on September 1, five after months I was enthroned, I spent the rest of the mourning period for my deceased mother also in this hall. Now on this 13th day of September, turning seventy-one, I am granting an audience to the subjects in the same hall, to revere the grace of her giving birth to me and bringing me up as well as to observe the proprieties among the sovereign and the subjects."

King Yeongjo's filial piety for his mother, Lady Sukbin Choi was very special even though she was a court attendant of a low social class working in a needlework room. It stoked up King Yeongjo's inferiority complex and political burden in the class-oriented Joseon Society that his mother was from a low social class. To overcome the complex, he took steps to upgrade the status of his diseased mother. On the year that he was enthroned, he built his mother's shrine and named it 'Shrine of Royal Lady Sukbin,' and paid a courteous visit to the shrine all of a sudden. After he came back to the palace, he even repeatedly refused a physical checkup by the royal clinic expressing his complaint about the ministers' negligence in paying respect to his deceased mother in the shrine.

King Yeongjo kept visiting Shrine of Lady Sukbin with unprecedented frequency. Then the shrine title was changed to Yuksangmyo Shrine in the 20th year of his reign, and the status was elevated further to Yuksanggung Palace in the 29th year of his rule.

Yuksanggung Palace was later incorporated into ✿Chilgung (Seven Palaces) in the west of Cheong wa dae (Korean presidential residence and office). Her grave was named Soryeongmyo Tomb in the 20th year of his reign, and upgraded to become the Soryeongwon Royal Concubine's Tomb in the 29th year of his reign. Whenever he upgraded the status of his mother's grave, an additional posthumous epithet was also offered.

✿ Chilgung : Chilgung is an agglomeration of seven shrines for biological mothers of Joseon kings including posthumously crowned kings, whose status was not queen but concubine. Since King Yeongjo built Yuksangung Palace for his mother Lady Sukbin Choi, six more spirit tablets were enshrined. The fact shows that filial piety was not limited to the queens as legal mothers of kings but also extended to biological mothers of kings regardless of their status as concubines.

6

Huijeongdang Hall
Dreaming of Bright Ruling

Huijeongdang (熙政堂) Hall stands east of Seonjeongjeon Hall. There are some features that show the building was remodeled into a Western style. The car-accessible porch was added to the southern corridor building so that the limousine of Emperor Sunjong could have easy access to the hall. The top part of the porch is adorned with a decorative frame surrounding the pillars,

The limousine of Emperor Sunjong pulling over at the porch of Huijeongdang (The National Museum of Korea collection)

Huijeongdang Hall seen through the porch

and the gilded *oyat* flower patterns of the imperial court of arms are also fixed. As the attached porch shuts down the access to the building currently, you can just peer into the inner court of Huijeongdang from outside.

To take a look at the inside of the Huijeongdang area, we should go around the building to the back. On the way to Daejojeon Hall through the site of Bogyeongdang, with Seonjeongjeon Hall on your left, you will notice the

Chinese character 'nyeong (寧)' on the west gable of Huijeongdang

Inner courtyard of Huijeongdang

Chinese character 'nyeong (寧 : meaning peace)' is engraved, if you carefully observe the west gable of Huijeongdang made of beautifully patterned brick walls. On your way out from Daejojeon Hall, on the opposite gable in the east you will see

Chinese character 'gang (康)' on the west gable of Huijeongdang

another Chinese character 'gang (康 : meaning health).' These characters are the evidence that Gangnyeongjeon (康寧殿), the king's bed chamber hall in Gyeongbokgung Palace was dismantled and the materials taken from the building were used to rebuild Huijeongdang in Changdeokgung.

141

Pine trees coated with snow in the inner courtyard of Huijeongdang

If you pass by the site of Bogyeongdang and continue to the back of Huijeongdang, you can see four-bay corridor buildings to the west and to the east of Huijeongdang, which connect Huijeongdang and Daejojeon (大造殿) Halls. The space between two halls is the backyard of Huijeongdang as well as the entrance area of Daejojeon at the same time. The eastern corridor also

The western corridor connecting Huijeongdang and Daejojeon

The rear of Huijeongdang seen from Seonpyeongmun of Daejojeon

leads to the front courtyard of Huijeongdang. Through the western corridor, you can reach Huijeongdang from the back side. It may feel strange to get access to a building from the rear part, but it is because the front part of Huijeongdang is blocked by the porch.

'Huijeong (熙政)' means 'harmonious and delightful governance.' Originally, Huijeongdang was built as a bed chamber hall for the king, however, it was used mainly as a council hall since Emperor Sunjong. The status of palace buildings was differentiated into eight classes according to the order of their importance and usage, such as *jeon, dang, hap, gak, jae, heon, ru,* and *jeong.* Even

though Huijeongdang belonged to the king's quarters, the suffix
'*dang*' meaning the lower status of a building than '*jeon*' was
applied in order to express practicing frugality and modesty,
which was the most important virtue in Confucian society. Its style
is also simple, having a single bracket between square pillars,
neither using multi brackets nor round pillars. It is a modest
15-bay building which is five-bay long and 3-bay wide. Initially
Jejeonggak Pavilion was there to the south of Huijeongdang, and
it was occupied by astronomical observation equipment called
Seongiokhyeong. According to *Gunggwolji* (Book of Palaces), there
was a pond in the east of Huijeongdang compound, and the lotus
flowers and the pips were especially pleasing during King
Hyeonjong's reign.

Part of *Chongseokjeong Jeolgyeongdo on* the eastern wall
(Changdeokgung Palace Office collection)

Part of *Geumgangsan Manmul Choseunggyeongdo* on the western wall
(Changdeokgung Palace Office collection)

However, after a big fire broke out in 1917 sweeping the whole inner court area of Changdeokgung, Gangnyeongjeon Hall of Gyeongbokgung Palace was dismantled and moved to the site of the burnt Huijeongdang. Due to the relocation the much bigger Gangnyeongjeon (a 55-bay building) to the site of the smaller 15-bay Huijeongdang, the newly restored Huijeongdang was much larger and made the existing compound look quite cramped. The roof ridge *yongmaru*, which the original Gangnyeongjeon did not have, was added using cement. The interior was also remodeled in the Western style. The middle three bays were made into a parlor, the west three bays into a conference room, and the east three bays were divided into small sections like a restroom and bathroom. In the big conference

147

area of the spacious wooden floor hall, Western style furniture was brought in. Paintings of Mt. Geumgang were attached to the east and the west walls. They are the works of *Geumgangsan Manmul Choseunggyeongdo* and *Chongseokjeong Jeolgyeongdo* by Kim Gyu-jin, whose pen name was Haegang, and he was the teacher of paintings and calligraphy for Imperial Crown Prince Uimin.

Carpet laid in Huijeongdang

Modern furniture displayed in Huijeongdang

149

7

Daejojeon Hall

Achieving a Great Work

Daejojeon Hall seen through Seonpyeongmun Gate
has no roof ridge *yongmaru*.

To the back side of Huijeongdang stands Seonpyeongmun (宣平門) Gate on steep stairs, which blocks public gaze, and beyond the gate Daejojeon (大造殿) Hall is located.

Have you noticed any peculiarity of Daejojeon, different from other buildings? Unlike the others, it has no roof ridge called a *yongmaru*. The top of the roof is just covered with curved

Daejojeon Hall

The western corridor building in Daejojeon

L-shaped roof tiles.

The roof without a ridge might have a functional meaning that it could be easily distinguished from a distance in an emergency, or it could have been thought that the smooth flow of vital energy from the nature into the king and the queen's dwelling space might be disturbed by installing a heavy artificial structure like a *yongmaru*.

'Daejo(大造)' means 'achieving a great work.' It is also interpreted as giving birth to a wise prince who will succeed to the throne for the long-lasting future of the kingdom because it is the queen's residence. Daejojeon is not only the queen's living

Deumu on the *woldae* of Daejojeon

space but also her office where she handled various official duties.

The queen was the head of all females in the nation as well as the mother of the people. She administered all the affairs related with female personnel, granting and removing official ranks for the *naemyeongbu* (inner female roster) and *oemyeongbu* (outer female roster). *Naemyeongbu* is from the first senior rank (1A) concubine called *bin* to the other court ladies and attendants who lived inside the palace. *Oemyeongbu* refers to the wives of the officials and royal relatives who lived outside the palace. When there was a national event, she granted an audience or held a banquet on the stone platform called *woldae* for *naemyeongbu* and *oemyeongbu.*

In historical dramas, scenes of a queen having frequent secret talks for conspiracy or gossiping with her relative menfolks in her residential area are grossly misleading about the roles of the queen. The queen could sometimes get involved in certain

155

political situations because of the faction that her birth family belonged to. Nevertheless, the queen and her birth family could not stand at the political forefront on principle, even if the person concerned with the situation were her father or brother. Other frequent themes in dramas describing a queen falling in jealousy and looking angrily at a concubine are also absurd. Joseon women were taught not to let their hard feelings show without reservation since Joseon was a fundamentally Confucian society where females

Heungbokheon Hall where the last cabinet meeting of the Great Han Empire was held.

were required to be submissive, patient, and docile. Accordingly, you should take into consideration that the situations are commonly exaggerated for dramatic effects and to generate interest in historical dramas.

From the time of Emperor Sunjong, Huijeongdang was used as his council hall, and the Emperor used the east bed chamber while the Empress used the west chamber of Daejojeon. In 1910,

156

the last cabinet meeting of the Great Han Empire was held in Heungbokheon (興福軒) Hall in the presence of Emperor Sunjong, and the Great Han Empire lost its sovereignty. Heungbokheon is the east wing attached to Daejojeon, where Emperor Sunjong met with Prince Imperials and ministers.

Due to a fire in 1917, when all the living quarters in the inner court were burned, the Japan are dismantled Gyotaejeon Hall in Gyeongbokgung and used the materials to rebuild Daejojeon. The fact that Japanese authorities rebuilt the burnt Huijeongdang and Daejojeon not with new building materials, but with the ones collected by dismantling buildings in Gyeongbokgung, which was the symbol of Royal authority, shows Japan's intentional purpose to wipe out the already ravaged dignity of the Joseon Royal Court.

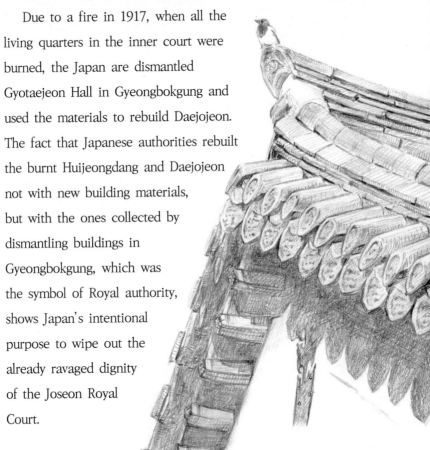

A magpie sitting on the roof of the west wing of Daejojeon

Gunhakdo (Painting of a Flock of Cranes) by Kim Eun-ho and four other painters in the 1920's on the western wall of Daejojeon

A chair

A bed and a chair

The bathtub and the floor pattern in the emperor's bathroom

The barber's worktable

158

Bonghwangdo (Painting of *Bonghwang*) by O Il-yeong and Yi Yong-wu in the 1920's on the eastern wall of Daejojeon

The pattern of the wooden floor hall

The ceiling

The wardrobe in a room of Daejojeon

The corridor of Daejojeon

A Mini Royal Kitchen

Out of Daejojeon and to a narrow western yard, there is a mini kitchen titled as 'Suragan (Royal Kitchen)'. When you hear the name 'Suragan', you are surely reminded of the big-scaled royal kitchen where Janggeum played an active role taking charge of royal meals as shown in the famous TV drama *Daejanggeum* (also exported under the title *Jewel in the Palace*). However, this tiny kitchen is far too small to be such a big royal kitchen. The interior walls are covered with tiles, and glass windows are installed. The upper part employs a window screen for ventilation. The iron gratings around the mesh windows are of the same kind still commonly seen in Europe. The kitchen has modern facilities such as a kitchen sink with water faucets, and an oven for baking cookies and preparing other Western dishes. The floor is covered with cement. It was built to prepare meals for Emperor Sunjong and Empress Sunjeonghyo 100 years ago.

Mesh windows in the kitchen

The interior of Royal Kitchen

Oven

Kitchen sink

Shelves

The door to Gyeonghungak Hall from the alley of Royal Kitchen

161

Passing by the alley of the Royal Kitchen, and going to the back side of Daejojeon, you can see Gyeonghungak (景薰閣) Hall. Being originally connected with Dajojeon through the inner corridors, Gyeonghungak was used as an annex where they could have a more comfortable rest.

'Gyeonghun (景薰)' or 'Gyeonggwang (景光)' means 'the scenery

Gyeonghungak

is heart warming.' Originally, it was a nine-bay long and four-bay wide two-story building. Its first floor was called Gyeonghungak Hall while the second floor was called Jinggwangnu Pavilion.

In *the Painting of the Eastern Palaces*, the roof of Gyeonghungak is painted in green like that of Seonjeongjeon, showing that Gyeonghungak was a very fancy building with blue-glazed roof tiles.

King Sunjo wrote a poem '*Jinggwangnusi* (Poem of Jinggwangnu Pavilion),' and recited it, "Surveying far and near from Jinggwangnu Pavilion, I see the fresh green of trees and plants filling the Capital with an auspicious sign. ··· Lifting the curtains of the pavilion, I feel clear fragrance float along the bright rays of sunshine."

Also in another writing of King Sunjo's, 'Jinggwangnumyeong' (On the name of Jinggwangnu Pavilion), he praised, "Gyeonghungak is the best for dwelling for all four seasons, for the first floor is good for autumn and winter while the second floor is pleasant for spring and summer." At that time, there were no tall buildings in front of the palace,

Bizarre stones in the backyard of Daejojeon

163

Stone-terraced flower beds are made in the rear garden.

and the scenery of the distant Mt. Namsan viewed from Jinggwangnu Pavilion on the second floor must have been very spectacular.

Gyeonghungak Hall was also burned by the fire in 1917. The Japanese government dismantled Mangyeongjeon Hall (built in 1874) which was located to the north of Jagyeongjeon Hall in Gyeongbokgung Palace, and used the building materials to restore the burnt Gyeonghungak, but only to complete the first floor.

Stone-terraced flower beds seen from Gyeonghungak

Stone-terraced Flower Beds
in the Rear Garden of Daejojeon

There are chimneys decorated in a flower-patterned brick wall style on the stone-terraced flower beds in the rear garden of Gyeonghungak and Daejojeon. Smoke flues from various rooms are installed underground and connected to one chimney, and the chimney is topped with many smoke vents. Detaching the chimneys that could be easily contaminated with soot, and

A chimney

Crane and deer pattern on the chimney

Chuyangmun Gate

decorating them in a beautiful flower-patterned wall style shows sense of beauty of the ancestors. Behind the garden are also flower-patterned brick walls telling that this area belonged to women.

Along the rear walls of Daejojeon compound are two exit gates of Chuyangmun (秋陽門) Gate and Cheonjangmun (天章門) Gate made toward the Rear Garden of Changdeokgung Palace. The arched doors add classical grace, and cranes known to live a thousand years holding an elixir plant in their mouth are engraved at either side of the arches. Outside Cheonjangmun Gate, the road to the Rear Garden of Changdeokgung is filled with lush greenery, and the air feels so fresh and cool even during the midsummer. To the left of the road is Gajeongdang Hall seated on an empty lot. It is a cozy and exquisite house built in a sunny place. 'Gajeong (嘉靖)' means 'beautiful and comfortable.' Since the house is not painted in the *Painting of the Eastern Palaces*, it is presumed to have been moved from Deoksugung at the end of the 19th century during the Japanese occupation period.

Royal azalea flowers dyeing the flower-patterned brick walls of Daejojeon

Cheonjangmun Gate to the Rear Garden of Changdeokgung

Now, you had better hurry a little to go to Seongjeonggak Hall. However, as the shortcut through Cheonjangmun Gate is currently blocked, you can go around the backyard of Daejojeon while taking a glance at Cheonghyanggak, and step down the stairs of Yeochunmun (麗春門) Gate on the east side of Daejojeon. The green arabesque design on the door posts catch your eyes.

A chimney and a pine tree next to Cheonghyanggak Hall

Designs on the chimneys

171

By now, you have understood why the name of the gate has a character 'chun (春)' which means 'spring.'

Like Geonchunmun Gate in Gyeongbokgung Palace, or Yeochunmun Gate in the east of Sungjeongjeon in Gyeonghuigung Palace, this Yeochunmun Gate in Daejojeon is also located on the east side. As the word 'yeochun (麗春)' stands for 'beautiful spring,' the stone-terraced flower beds on the east side of Daejojeon and Huijeongdang are planted with so many *aengdu* (Korean cherry) trees that we actually feel the smell of spring at the dazzling beauty of those spring flowers.

Arabesque design on the door posts of Yeochunmun   The water inlet on the wall next to Yeochunmun

When the azalea and *aengdu* flowers are in bloom,
the rear garden of Daejojeon seems to be stretching
its arms greeting spring.

Beyond the walls of Yeochunmun Gate, Zelkovas in the Rear Garden are in their fall finery.

While diverting our attention to the beauty of the flowers, we naturally pass through Donginmun Gate, and get to the front side of Huijeongdang Hall. Finally, we have come to the outside of the living quarters after browsing here and there in the inner court area. The blue-glazed roof of Seonjeongjeon down below looks rather more conspicuous from here. The porch with the decorative pillar frame at the front of Huijeongdang Hall also looks brilliant.

Aengdu trees coated with snow below Donginmun Gate

After browsing around Daejojeon area, we get to go outside through the gate between Seongjeonggak and Huijeongdang.

175

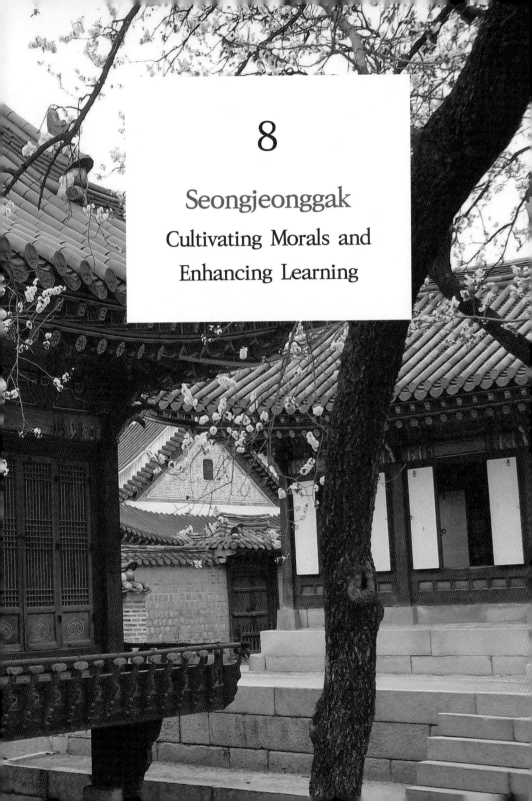

8

Seongjeonggak
Cultivating Morals and
Enhancing Learning

Looking forward to flower blossoming April under
the pavilion of Bochunjeong on a snowy day

Seongjeonggak Hall and Royal Clinic

Seongjeonggak (誠正閣) Hall is right next to Huijeongdang. With the name of the entrance 'Yeonghyeonmun (迎賢門) Gate,' which literally means 'a gate of welcoming a wise man,' this place reveals itself as a learning hall. Seongjeonggak originally belonging to the crown prince's residence was where the king or the crown prince held a royal lecture (*gyeongyeon*) or a learning session (*seoyeon*). 'Seongjeong (誠正)' was extracted from a phrase in Chinese Confusian Classic, the *Great Learning* (大學), which insists that a ruler has to govern the people after morally cultivating himself first with sincerity and right mind.

The entrance to Seongjeonggak, Yeonghyeonmun Gate

When we get inside through Yeonghyeonmun Gate, we can see two buildings in the south with their respective signboards, '*Johwa-eoyak* (調和御藥)' and '*Boho-seonggung* (保護聖躬).' They all mean preparing good medicine for the king. By the way, did you happen to

179

Royal Clinic with two signboards of '*Johwa-eoyak* (調和御藥)' and '*Boho-seonggung* (保護聖躬)' and a medicine mortar on the yard

notice that only the three characters 'eo (御)' and 'seonggung (聖躬)' among the characters are lifted up higher than the others. As they are the characters that mean 'king,' they are naturally placed higher than the others according to propriety. The medicine mortar laid on the yard tells us that this area was once briefly used as the Royal Clinic.

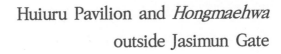

Huiuru Pavilion and *Hongmaehwa* outside Jasimun Gate

Attached to Seongjeonggak Hall, there is a loft with two name plaques. The one in the south reads 'Bochunjeong (報春亭),' and the other one in the east 'Huiuru (喜雨樓).' The word 'huiu' which means 'delightful rain' was used frequently as the name of a building or a pavilion in Joseon Palaces. In fact, even in the Rear Garden of Changdeokgung is another pavilion named Huiujeong

Snow-white apricot blossoms over the wall of Huiuru Pavilion

to the west of Gyujanggak Pavilion. Huiuru in the Seongjeonggak area was named so as a compliment, when a much-awaited rain finally fell after King Jeongjo's great anxiety, on the day that they finished repairing the pavilion.

In front of Huiuru Pavilion are old apricot trees and persimmon trees. You would have a jolly good time enjoying flower-viewing under the apricot trees on a fine spring day. Besides, there is also another beautiful spring flower outside the wall.

Jasimun Gate is the east gate of Seongjeonggak area, and there is a *hongmaehwa* tree (red winter plum) in front of the gate, which is said to have been sent from a Chinese emperor of the Ming Dynasty. If it were true, the tree must have been more than 400 years old. That may be the reason why it looks so feeble. Anyway, beautiful *hongmaehwa* flowers blossom every spring and present a grand sight around the wall outside Jasimun Gate. Just imagine the sight of the master of the house sitting on the loft of Huiuru and greeting every spring heralded by the *hongmaehwa*.

Hongmaehwa blossoms casting the reflections on the wall

Multi-ply *hongmaehwa* in front of Jasimun Gate

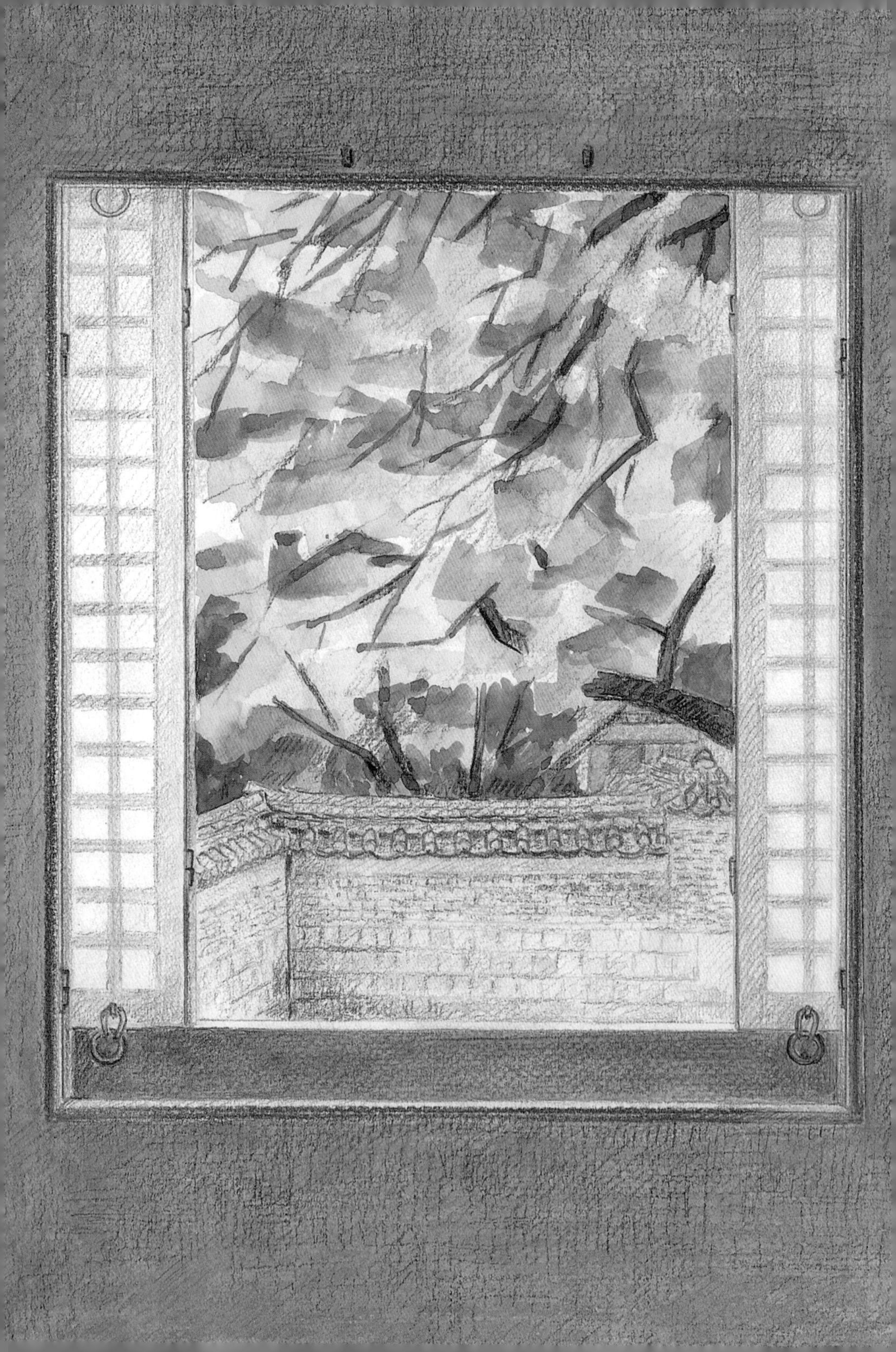

Gwanmulheon Hall, Crown Prince's Study Hall

Behind Seongjeonggak is Gwanmulheon (觀物軒) Hall on top of the steps. As 'gwanmul (觀物)' means 'to observe matters and things,' we can assume that this hall was used for learning. Actually it was a study hall for the king and the crown prince.

'Jiphui (緝熙)' written on the name plaque means 'to wish to have a good character that shines for a long time,' or 'to succeed to the old things and to broaden them.'

Gwanmulheon Hall

185

Judging from the handwriting which is not so flowing, the name plaque must have been written by a child who had learned how to write just for a short period of time. The plaque says that it was written by 'the King' in the sexagenary year of gapja (1864), when King Gojong was 13 years old. As he was newly enthroned as king, the meaning of 'Jiphui (緝熙)' can be interpreted as expressing his volition to succeed to the previous king's achievements and broaden them. Gwanmulheon was the very place where Emperor Sunjong was born, and also was the stronghold for the Enlightenment Party during the Gapsin Coup in 1884.

Spring scenes in the backyard of Gwanmulheon

On a hot summer day, when the doors of Gwanmulheon are open to the public, I wish you would sit on the wooden floor and enjoy the cool breezes as well as the shade offered by the apricot trees in the yard.

Autumn scenes in the backyard of Gwanmulheon

186

Fuel holes and a chimney to the west of Gwanmulheon

Seunghwaru Pavilion seen beyond the wall of Gwanmulheon

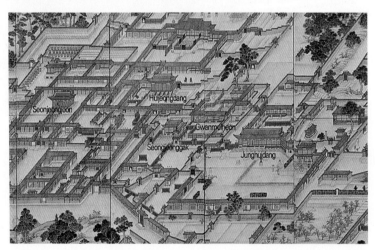

According to the *Painting of the Eastern Palaces*, Junghuidang Hall was installed with various astronomical instruments in the yard.

Junghuidang Hall, a Place to the Groom Crown Prince as the Next King

Beyond the eastern wall of Seongjeonggak area Junghuidang (重熙堂) Hall was once located, which was the crown prince's residence. On the *Painting of the Eastern Palaces*, we can confirm that it was equipped with various astronomical instruments for the education of the crown prince. Junghuidang was built by King Jeongjo in 1782 (the sixth year of his reign) for his first son, Crown Prince Munhyo. However, since the crown

The site of Junghuidang Hall has become the shortcut to the Rear Garden of Changdeokgung.

189

Chilbunseo Corridor and Samsamwa Pavilion

prince died at five, it was used as a council hall by King Jeongjo, and later by Crown Prince Hyomyeong when he acted as regent.

The Junghuidang site to the east of Seongjeonggak area has now been turned into a broad road leading to the Rear Garden. Only the eastern part of Junghuidang area including Seunghwaru Pavilion (also called as Sojuhamnu Pavilion: crown prince's library), Samsamwa (the gazebo), and Chilbunseo (the corridor) is remaining,

190

Seunghwaru Pavilion

and helps us figure out what the original shape was like. When we stand on the site of Junghuidang, the small hexagonal gazebo seen through *maehwa* trees is Samsamwa, and the connected corridor on the left is Chilbunseo. They were the structures originally connected to Junghuidang Hall.

Seunghwaru Pavilion is conjectured to have been the library of the crown prince, and there used to be a room called Uisingak on its first floor. The second floor was called Sojuhamnu (Little Juhamnu Pavilion). Considering that the Royal Library was called Juhamnu, Sojuhamnu must have been the reading and resting area for the crown prince. During the reign of King Heonjong, the name was changed to Seunghwaru, and the books classified in accordance with the categories were stored in the pavilion.

A small wicket door and the flower-patterned brick wall of Seunghwaru Pavilion

Leaving the Seongjeonggak area behind, on your way to Nakseonjae Complex, if you stop for a moment and find the spot where you can see the whole view of the complex and its rear garden area, it will give you the best perspective from which you can see the most beautiful the Nakseonjae complex from outside. The clusters of multi-stemmed

Branches of weeping cherry flower tree drooping over the wall of Seunghwaru

pine trees in front of Seunghwaru, and the diverse but well-harmonized walls and roof lines show outstandingly aesthetic sense. It will be really impressive to have the whole view without missing anything including the distant Sangryangjeong Pavilion and even all the patterns designed on the brick walls between the living quarters and the rear garden area.

The spot that commands the whole view of Seunghwaru Pavilion
and the Nakseonjae Complex

9

Nakseonjae Complex

Running into Destined Love

King Heonjong's Love in Nakseonjae

Originally, Changdeokgung and Changgyeonggung was bordered by the Geonyangmun Gate, and the Nakseonjae (樂善齋) Complex beyond Geonyangmun Gate had belonged to the living quarters of Changgyeonggung Palace. The Nakseonjae Complex is comprised of Nakseonjae, Seokbokheon (錫福軒), and Sugangjae (壽康齋) Halls. King Taejong constructed Suganggung Palace (1418)

Jangnakmun Gate seen from the loft of Nakseonjae

197

to reside in after he abdicated his throne in favor of King Sejong. Later, King Seongjong built Changgyeonggung (昌慶宮) Palace on the site of Suganggung. In the 13th year of King Heonjong's reign (1847), he built his private living quarters in the area, and afterwards it became the very place where the royal descendants of the Joseon Dynasty spent the last years of their lives.

When a fire broke out in Gyeongbokgung in 1876, King Gojong used Nakseonjae as his council hall while taking care of state affairs in Junghuidang. Emperor Sunjong also used Nakseonjae when Huijeongdang and Daejojeon Halls of Changdeokgung were burnt down by a fire in 1917. 'Nakseon (樂善)' means 'to take delight in goodness.' 'Goodness' was considered the prime virtue of a noble man.

The entrance of Nakseonjae is Jangnakmun (長樂門) Gate. The word 'Jangnak (長樂)' was derived from Jangnakgung Palace where the Queen Mother of the West (Xi Wangmu) in a Chinese legend lived, which means that this place is a Taoistic fairyland where hermits live. From the signature engraved on the left corner of the name plaque, the characters seem to be on engraving of Regent Heungson's caligraphy. Passing through the gate, we can notice that the middle part of the threshold is grooved. It is a trace that the officials of the rank of junior second degree (2B) or higher frequently visited the house carried in a mono-wheel sedan chair. The view of Sangryangjeong Pavilion in its rear

Name plaques of 'Nakseonjae' and 'Bosodang'

garden seen through Jangnakmun gate is outstandingly picturesque.

Under the eave of Nakseonjae Hall is a name plaque in the east that reads 'Bosodang (寶蘇堂).' Bosodang is King Heonjong's reception room for male guests. The word 'boso' means 'to treasure Su Shi (蘇軾)' who was a Chinese poet and artist whose pen name was Dongpo during the Northern Song Dynasty. Weng Fang-gang (翁方綱) of Qing China admired Su Shi so much that he named his house 'Bosojae,' and Kim Jeong-hui of the Joseon Dynasty also entitled his house 'Bosojae.'

The corridor and Jangnakmun Gate seen from
the backyard of Nakseonjae

Simple, but Elegant Aesthetic Sense of Beauty

Nakseonjae is an austere house without the multi-colored *dancheong* paintwork. If Nakseonjae adopted any decoration to mention, it would be various styles of door gratings. The beautiful shadows of the geometric patterns cast on the floor through the sunlit window paper demonstrate the elegant aesthetic value of this house. The composition of space formed

Railings along the corridors of Nakseonjae

by the full moon-shaped door in the room is tastefully refined even compared to the modern sense of beauty.

When it comes to referring to decoration, we cannot fail to mention the symbolism of the Taoistic hermit world hidden in various ornaments. If you take a careful look at the outer bottom frames of the loft and corridors, you will notice that wooden boards in the shape of clouds are attached. They are nothing but scraps of wooden panels, but adding them gives a metaphor, which turns the loft above the boards into a Taoistic world above the clouds, and the Confucian scholar reading a book in the room into a Taoistic hermit.

Taking after his brilliant father (Crown Prince Hyomyeong), the master of Nakseonjae, King Heonjong was well versed in writing calligraphy, and took pleasure in reading as well as maintained a keen interest in paintings and calligraphic works. He always praised King Yeongjo's frugal life style, and tried to follow his example. In that context, he did not paint the Nakseonjae Complex with *dancheong*, being extremely weary of extravagance. Therefore, you can feel the restrained taste of King Heonjong all throughout the house. Nevertheless, we should not miss the elevated sense of aesthetics that fills up the inside of the moderation.

Bat designs on the railings of corridors

Various patterns of door gratings in Nakseonjae

A full moon-shaped door in Nakseonjae

Patterns of a Tortoise Shell and Broken Ice

A flower-patterned brick wall means a wall that is decorated with various patterns. The patterns are metaphors containing the earnest wishes of the ancestors.

The eastern wall of Nakseonjae is decorated with running patterns of a tortoise shell. As a tortoise lives very long, it stands for longevity. It is also called 'a grate pattern' as it looks like a grill, which means filtering all the evils out before they enter the house.

Tortoise shell patterns on the eastern wall of Nakseonjae

A broken ice pattern under the loft

On the low wall under the loft of Nakseonjae is a broken ice pattern that reminds us of Mondrian's composition works. It is also called 'a bamboo firework pattern' as the cracking noise of bamboo firework in ancient China was similar to the sound of ice cracking. There was a superstition that the noise could drive away evil spirits. By the way, why in the world is the broken ice pattern made on this wall? The answer is found when you turn to the back of the wall, and find the fuel holes made to heat the *ondol* rooms. Ice is another form of water, which naturally symbolizes warding off any chance of a fire.

A flower-patterned brick wall with tortoise shell patterns in Nakseonjae

Designs on the flower-patterned walls of Nakseonjae and its rear garden

A fret pattern and a double ring pattern: A fret pattern is a shape that lightening strikes, and is also called a character 'ah (亞) pattern.' Sometimes, the straight lines are modified into the shapes of knots in the corners or along the outlines of the pattern. The double ring pattern has many overlapping rings, which means infinite eternity having neither beginning nor end.

The pattern of '卍 (ten thousand)': This pattern was used rather for its beautiful composition made by the various transformations of the lines than for its Buddhist connotation. The pattern means fullness, or expresses the logic of the harmony of heaven and earth.

Auspicious character patterns: Main characters that were used in the decorative palace brick walls were 'su (壽: long life),' 'bok (福: blessing),' 'gangnyeong (康寧: physical health and mental peace),' 'hui (囍: joy of happy occasions),' 'man (萬: long time),' and 'se (歲: long time),' which contain their wish for enjoying a heathy and blessed long life.

Elixir plants of eternal life and grapes: Bunches of grapes in clusters usually decorated in female quarters mean fertility, and the elixir plants of eternal life similar to Lingzhi mushroom stand for long life without sickness.

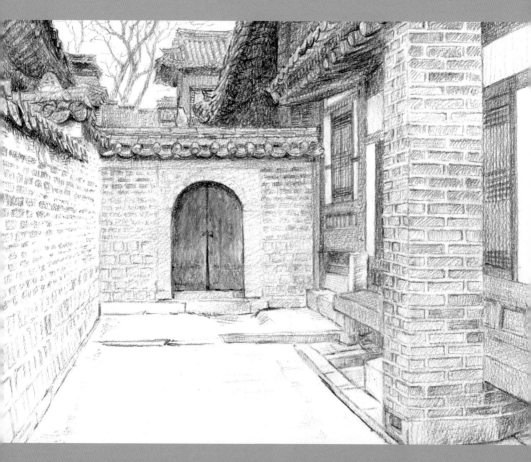

A wicket gate in the alley to Seokbokheon Hall from Nakseonjae

Seokbokheon Hall, Living Quarters for Females

Seokbokheon (錫福軒) located to the east of Nakseonjae is a bijou residence for females with a cozy courtyard. The railings of the corridors are also decorated with pretty designs of a gourd bottle, a lotus leaf, and a bat.

When King Heonjong took Lady Gyeongbin Kim of Sunhwagung as his royal concubine, he built Seokbokheon Hall for her. 'Seokbok (錫福)' means 'to bestow blessings.' She was taken from the wish of the royal court to have a crown prince to succeed to the throne, however, the wish ended in vain as King Heonjong passed away at the young age of 23 in the 15th year of his reign, barely two years since he took Lady Gyeongbin Kim.

The courtyard of Seokbokheon

The corridor railings of Seokbokheon

Designs of a gourd bottle and a lotus leaf on the corridor railings

A Woman who stole King Heonjong's Heart,
Lady Gyeongbin Kim

Constructing a new residential complex in the Nakseonjae
area was related to King Heonjong's taking a royal concubine
named Lady Gyeongbin Kim (also called as Lady Sunhwagung). King
Heonjong is the son of Crown Prince Hyomyeong. When his
father Crown Prince Hyomyeong died young at 22, King
Heonjong (r.1834~1849) was enthroned when he was eight,
succeeding his grandfather King Sunjo. In the third year of his
reign in 1837, he married Queen Hyohyeon. She died at sixteen
without leaving a child. In the next year in 1844, King Heonjong
married his second wife, Queen Hyojeong. Then three years later
in 1847, Lady Gyeongbin Kim was taken as his concubine. She
received unprecedentedly preferential treatment compared to
previous royal concubines. She was from a noble family, and had
already reached the final round in the three-stage formal
screening process for the selection of the second queen in 1844.

According to the norms of the time, the queen selection
process was considered a matter in the queen dowager's charge,
therefore, the king was not supposed to participate in the
process. However, as King Heonjong was already 18, expressing

his strong will to decide his own spouse, he insisted on presenting himself in the procedure. On the site, King Heonjong got a crush on Lady Gyeongbin Kim, but to his great disappointment, the Queen dowager selected Queen Hyojeong as his second wife.

After patiently waiting for three years, King Heonjong pleaded with his grandmother on the necessity to have an heir, as there had been no child between him and Queen Hyojeong with that time. Queen Dowager Sunwon was persuaded and delivered a message written in Hangeul (Korean alphabets) to *Bincheong* (ministers' waiting and meeting room), ordering them to select a royal concubine and let the Royal line be carried on. King Heonjong could finally take his beloved Lady Gyeongbin Kim as his concubine in the 13th year of his reign in 1847.

Selected under those circumstances, she received unprecedentedly respectful treatment from the royal court. We can confirm the fact from a set of books written by her, *Sunhwagung Cheopcho* (Notebooks of Lady Sunhwagung). The books are surveys of the proper clothing and ornaments for the ladies of the royal court according to occasions such as the royal ancestors' anniversaries, major national holidays and seasonal festive days. *Sunhwagung Cheopcho* is meaningful in that it enables us to trace the different holiday customs of the royal court that had faded away.

214

A lady wearing a ceremonial wig and ornamental hairpins

In other words, *Sunhwagung Cheopcho* was a total fashion guidebook for the ladies of the day. It describes in detail the kinds of fabrics for each season and styles of clothing according to colors, and catalogs of ornaments and accessories are also recorded from point to point. The contents of the books also verify that Lady Gyeongbin Kim (Lady Sunhwagung) was treated every bit as specially well as the queen was.

Unfortunately, though, her blissful romance did not last very long. She was bereaved of King Heonjong when he was 23 in 1849 (the 15th year of his reign), and she had not produced his heir yet. Queen Hyojeong, who was completely turned away from her husband because of her rival, Lady Gyeongbin Kim, whom the queen might well feel jealous of, kept ironically good terms with her for many, many years after their common lover, King Heonjong's death. Queen Hyojeong (1831~1903) lived to 73, and Lady Gyeongbin Kim (1832~1907) died at 76. When she passed away, Emperor Gojong lamented deeply, wrote a eulogy for her, and ordered to give a special assistance for her funeral arrangements.

Small servants' quarters in the alley to Sugangjae Hall from Seokbokheon

Sugangjae (壽康齋) Hall lies to the east of Seokbokheon. 'Sugang (壽康)' means 'to enjoy a healthy and long life.' It was the living quarters of Queen Sunwon (King Sunjo's wife), who was the grandmother of King Heonjong. Unlike Nakseonjae or Seokbokheon, Sugangjae is finished with *dancheong*. If you take a closer look, you can find the faded colors of *dancheong* on the

Sugangjae Hall

217

From outside the eastern wall of Sugangjae, you can reach the rear garden through the steps and the door.

pillars and rafters.

Long ago in the earlier period of Joseon, here used to stand Suganggung Palace where King Taejong dwelt after he abdicated the throne in favor of King Sejong. King Sejong's son, King Danjong also stayed here until he was exiled to Yeongwol by his uncle King Sejo. Thereafter it became the very place where King Sejo died.

The storage door of Sugangjae

A decorative wall with *maehwa* design next to a wicket gate in the back of Sugangjae

The outer decorative wall with grape design

221

Stone-terraced flower beds in the back yard of Nakseonjae

The Rear Garden of Nakseonjae

While the living quarters of the Nakseonjae complex are affiliated with each other, each residence is sectioned by walls, ensuring an independent space. The back yards leading to the small mounds are also divided by low walls, not tall enough to isolate each other. Through wicket gates, their back yards are all connected with each other forming a whole rear garden area. The rear garden functions not only as a small mound surrounding

Snow-covered scenery of stone-terraced flower beds in the back of Nakseonjae

a commoner's house, which embraces the house snugly from behind but also as a perfect space to relax. Each residence has its own pavilion in its rear garden, and they bespeak the owner's disposition wanting to appreciate the serenity of nature in a highly elevated space.

The back yards of Nakseonjae, Seokbokheon, and Sugangjae Halls are mutually accessible through tiered stone terraces. Flower trees are planted on the terraces similar to the flower beds of Daejojeon Hall through which they could enjoy four seasons. In addition, the beauty of the chimneys erected here and there on the tiers is another charm of Korean traditional architecture.

Spring has come to the stone-terraced flower beds in Nakseonjae.

A chimney decorated with honeysuckle designs and the character 'su (壽)' pattern

The walls built on top of the stone terraces separate the rear garden area from the living quarters, and the small gates along the walls serve as the entrances to the rear garden. The various decorative patterns on the walls, as well as the lovely wicket gates in between them, compose a very exquisite canvas, and each space that the wall divides creates a unique atmosphere.

From the bizarre rocks in the stone pedestals that make you imagine being in the heart of the mountains to the small yard around each pavilion arousing sweetness in your mind, the rear garden of the Nakseonjae complex displays a dignified sense of beauty.

226

Embracing the Scenery of the Heaven into the Heart

In the backyard of Nakseonjae, there is a stone pot on which an oddly formed rock is placed. On the hexagonal stone pot is inscribed 'Soyeongju (小瀛州)' which means 'Little Yeongju.' Yeongju refers to one of three Taoist mountains as well as Bongrae and Bangjang. Legend has it that it was located in the middle of the eastern sea, where Taoistic hermits live and elixir plants grow. On the bizarre shaped rock on the pot is engraved 'Unbiongnip (雲飛玉立),' which symbolizes that this place is a Taoist world where clouds fly and jade stones stand.

Next to the 'Soyeongju' rock, on a

A stone pot inscribed with 'Soyeongju (小瀛州)'

An oddly formed rock engraved with 'Unbiongnip (雲飛玉立)'

big stone cistern is inscribed 'Geumsayeonji (琴史硯池)' in seal script, which implies that the master of the house enjoys playing *geomungo* lute and reading history books in the house. Even though the oddly shaped rocks and stone cisterns are appreciable on their own, they also give you another way of enjoying the nature.

A stone cistern engraved with 'Geumsayeonji (琴史硯池)'

The term '*chagyeong* (借景)' literally means to borrow the scenery. Rather than appreciating the visual images, you can embrace the imaginary mountain into your heart from the oddly shaped rocks. You can plant lotus flowers in the stone cistern and enjoy their beauty, but the delectation that you get from the reflection of the scenery is also special. Not by moving a whole mountain to enjoy, but by placing a small oddly shaped rock in the yard, you can embrace the mountain in your heart.

Sangryangjeong Pavilion and Manwolmun Gate

Sangryangjeong is a hexagonal pavilion in the rear garden of Nakseonjae Hall. It was originally called Pyeongwonnu Pavilion, and its beauty is comparable to that of Hyangwonjeong Pavilion in Gyeongbokgung. The ceiling is treated with a hexagonal surface fully decorated with many auspicious designs symbolizing wealth · longevity · fecundity, such as bat · peach · horned orange · blue

Designs of a pair of cranes and blue dragon on the ceiling of Sangryangjeong Pavilion

Sangryangjeong Pavilion and Manwolmun Gate

dragon and a pair of cranes. At the back of the pavilion is a long corridor storage building, where lots of books and paintings were discovered in 1969.

The rear gardens of Nakseonjae Hall and Seunghwaru Pavilion are connected with each other with the wall in between. The charming mood felt when passing through the Manwolmun Gate (Full moon-shaped gate) dividing the sections of Sangryangjeong and Seunghwaru is quite special. You reach the Taoist fairyland watching the full moon in the sky passing through another moon on the earth. It is also a way of borrowing the scenery, '*chagyeong* (借景).'

The view of Mt. Bugak seen through Manwolmun Gate is awesome.

Hanjeongdang Hall and Chwiunjeong Pavilion

Hanjeongdang (閒靜堂) Hall is an annex of Seokbokheon located in its rear garden. According to the 'Donggwol-dohyeong,' the *Map of the Eastern Palaces* made around 1907, as the site was empty then, it can be assumed that Hanjeongdang was built later during the Japanese ruling period. The house is added with different features from traditional *hanok* (Korean style house), such as glass windows and tiled stylobate.

Hanjeongdang Hall

In the yard of Hanjeongdang are placed several pieces of oddly formed rock which catch your eye not only for their formative features but also for their stone pedestals with ornately carved designs using a traditional technique. In Korean traditional landscaping, there is an expression, 'to embellish the garden with oddly shaped rocks.' It suggests that the ancients took much labor in collecting those rocks to invite and enjoy the mountains inside the house.

Chwiunjeong Pavilion viewed from Sugangjae Hall

Chwiunjeong (翠雲亭) Pavilion of Sugangjae residence is the oldest building in this complex. Built in the 12th year of King Sukjong's reign (1686), it is also painted in the *Painting of the Eastern Palaces* in which the Nakseonjae Complex was not depicted yet. Chwiunjeong is a house with both wooden floor halls and *ondol* rooms equipped with fuel holes on the east side. As the elevation of the house is quite high, you can see the distant Changgyeonggung Palace over the low wall to the east, and the Hamchunwon Garden site way beyond the palace. Hamchunwon, currently located in the grounds of Seoul National University Hospital, was the eastern garden of Changgyeonggung Palace.

233

The backyard of Seokbokheon Hall overlooked from Hanjeongdang

The Tale of the Last Royal Family

Unlike the other living quarters in Changdeokgung Palace, the Nakseonjae Complex was inhabited by the royal descendants of the Joseon Dynasty until recently. When a fire broke out in 1917, and burned Huijeongdang and Daejojeon Halls in the inner court area, Emperor Sunjong and Empress Sunjeonghyo used the Nakseonjae complex as their temporary residence.

Emperor Sunjong and the Empress Sunjeonghyo

The Empress Sunjeonghyo was the last empress, who was invested as the second lawful crown princess, and was upgraded to empress when Sunjong was enthroned as the emperor of the Great Han Empire. After Emperor Sunjong passed away, she resided in Nakseonjae. When the Korean War broke out in 1950, she could not but stay in Nakseonjae without being able to flee due to the indifference of the President Rhee Syng-man regime. However, during the January 4 retreat in 1951,

235

From the left, Imprerial Crown Prince Uimin, Emperor Sunjong, the abdicated Emperor Gojong, Empress Sunjeonghyo, and Princess Deokhye

she fled to Busan with the help of the U.S. Army. After the cease-fire, she returned to Seoul, only to be prohibited from living in Nakseonjae by President Rhee Syng-man. She stayed in Suinjae Hall in Jeongneung-dong until she could finally return to Seokbokheon Hall of Nakseonjae in 1960.

Empress Sunjeonghyo was so absorbed in Buddhism that she even received the Buddhist name Daejiweol. Despite her old age, she was not only devoted to studying Buddhist scriptures and English but also learned to play the piano. Empress Sunjeonghyo passed away in February 1966 at 72 in Seokbokheon Hall. People say that she tried not to lose her dignity as the State Mother, and embraced the royal family members who were torn asunder, giving them warm treatment.

236

Nakseonjae Hall was also inhabited by Imperial Crown Princess Uimin (also known as Madame Yi Bang-ja) from when she returned to Korea in 1963 until she died in 1989. Imperial Crown Prince Uimin (also known as King Yeongchin) had been forcibly taken to Japan at the young age of 11 in 1907, and returned to Korea at 56 with a sick body in 1963. He fought against cerebral thrombosis for 7 years receiving treatments at St. Mary's Hospital of The Catholic University in Seoul, but passed away on May 1 in 1970 on the same day he returned to Nakseonjae for his final rest. Emperor Gojong's youngest daughter Princess Deokhye also lived in Sugangjae Hall in the Nakseonjae complex after she returned to Korea from Japan in 1962 until she died in 1989. Nine days after her death, Imperial Crown Princess Uimin, Princess Deokhye's half sister-in-law, also ended her life in Nakseonjae.

A Princess of Misfortune, Deokhye

The abdicated Emperor Gojong had his youngest daughter Priness Deokhye when he was sixty with his royal concubine, Lady Boknyeongdang Yang, on May 25, 1912. Having his daughter at the old age, he loved her so much and Prince Deokhye received much affection from the royal family. Her name was formally enlisted in the Imperial Genealogy in 1917. In an effort to prevent the Japanese colonial government from forcing her to marry a Japanese, Gojong tried to make her engaged to Kim Jang-han, a nephew of Gojong's chamberlain, Kim Hwang-jin in

Princess Deokhye when attending Gakushuin in Tokyo after she was taken to Japan

1919, but only to fail. Then the abdicated Emperor Gojong met his sudden demise on January 21 in the same year.

When Princess Deokhye was five in 1916, a kindergarten was established for her education in Junmyeongdang Hall of Deoksugung Palace, and Gyoguchi Sadako and Jang Ok-sik were appointed as her governesses. Afterwards, she attended Hinode Elementary School for the children of Japanese in Seoul. Meanwhile she was being called 'Agissi of Lady Boknyeongdang' meaning 'a royal baby of Lady Boknyeongdang.' On May 4 in 1921, she was officially titled as Princess Deokhye.

However, after the death of her father Gojong, the Joseon royal court, which had already been deprived of its sovereignty by Japan, could not protect Princess Deokhye from the Japanese government's maneuvers. Under the pretense that they needed to educate the Japanese Imperial family members in Japan, she was forcibly taken to Japan in April 1925 when she was only thirteen, and was made to attend Gakushuin in Tokyo. It must have been a tremendous mental ordeal for her to overcome loneliness and psychological anguish.

When her half brother, Emperor Sunjong got critically ill, she returned home briefly, but after Emperor Sunjong passed away, she was not allowed to attend the national funeral and was sent back to Japan on May 10. Only on the first anniversary of his death, she could participate in the ceremony in 1927. Moreover, when her birth mother Lady Boknyeongdang Yang got seriously ill, she returned home on April 22 in 1929, however, when her mother died on May 30, Princess Deokhye was prohibited by Japan from wearing mourning attire as a mourner, and again was sent back to Japan. Previously, when she returned home at the time of Emperor Sunjong's death, she was also not allowed to meet her mother. Therefore, since she was taken to Japan at 13, she was unable to see her mother alive for four years. Due to the shock and despair, she began to show signs of sleepwalking from the spring of 1930, and was moved to her half brother Imperial Crown Prince Uimin's residence for treatment. She was diagnosed with dementia praecox (schizophrenia).

When her symptoms seemed to have improved in the next year, she was made to marry to Count Sō Takeyuki, a descendant of Sō clan that governed Tsushima Island, as already arranged according to the Japanese colonial government's political motivation. She gave birth to a daughter Jeonghye (正惠 : Masae) in the next year. However, as her illness worsened from her marriage, she was hospitalized in the Psychiatric Asylum of Matsuzawa Hospital in Tokyo in 1946. After she spent many years in mental clinics, she and Sō Takeyuki finally got divorced in 1955. Although there are different views on the exact time of the divorce such as 1951 and 1953, it was in 1955 according to Imperial Crown Princess Uimin's book, *Heulleo Ganeundaero* (Going with the Flow). Her only daughter Jeonghye also suffered from an unhappy marriage, and disappeared in a mountainous area of Southern Alps of Japan leaving her will. (There exists an opinion that she committed a suicide.)

After the liberation of Korea, the regine of the first president

240

of the Republic of Korea, Rhee Syng-man turned a cold shoulder to the royal descendants living in Japan, and disapproved of their returning to Korea. Later, owing to the solicitude of President Park Chung-hee, she returned to her homeland at last on January 26, 1962. On the day she arrived, she met her half sister-in-law Empress Sunjeonghyo in Nakseonjae, but by that time, she could hardly talk, suffering from aphasia. Nevertheless, only the Nakseonjae complex in Changdeokgung Palace might have given her some slight consolation after all her tragic life as the last imperial princess of the Great Han Empire. At the age of 78, she ended her sorrowful life in Sugangjae Hall on April 22 in 1989, and went to her eternal rest in her tomb located at the rear of her father Emperor Gojong's tomb, Hongleung in Gyeonggi-do Province.

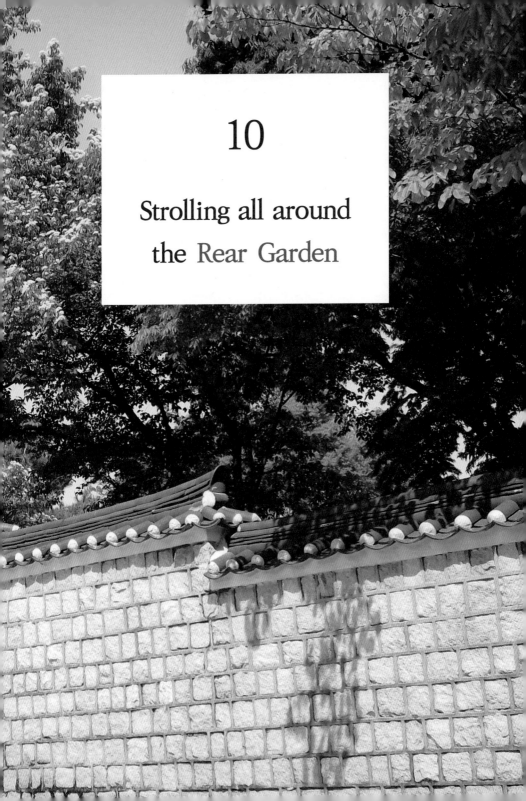

10

Strolling all around the Rear Garden

Greenery casts a shadow over the path leading to the Rear Garden

The Path that Leads You to the Rear Garden

The Rear Garden of Changdeokgung Palace was more widely known as 'Secret Garden' for a long time. Its name, Secret Garden, came from the name of the office which was in charge of the Rear Garden in the last years of the Joseon Dynasty. The name Secret Garden first appeared in the first article dated December 30th, 1903 from *Emperor Gojong's Annals*. It said, "Secret Garden (祕苑) undertakes a job of tending and managing the Rear Garden."

According to the second article dated April 17th, 1908 from *Emperor Sunjong's Annals*, "His Majesty went out to the Secret Garden and enjoyed shooting arrows at the targets. Lots of officials attended his Majesty on the archery tour." Afterwards, the garden was open to the public during Japanese rule and it began to be called the 'Secret Garden.'

Currently the route to the Rear Garden begins at the broad road outside the wall of Gwanmulheon Hall. The path which was built in the 1960s by Park Chung-hee's military regime is said to be the shortcut running to the rear garden. Since the Joseon Dynasty, Changdeokgung has had several routes toward the Rear

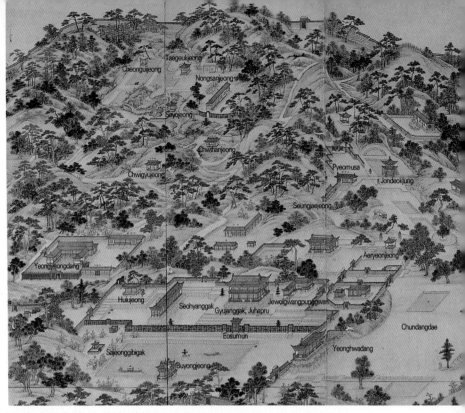

The Rear Garden section of the *Painting of the Eastern Palaces*

Garden. Cheonjangmun Gate behind Gyeonghungak Hall or some small gates over the stone terraces all lead to the Rear Garden. Now, the wide road starting from the Hamyangmun Gate has become the nearest and most convenient route.

However, I feel something is missing when it comes to appreciating true beauty as well as classic taste. That is because seeking after only 'nearness' or 'convenience' can run low on its charms. Nevertheless, you cannot help but acknowledge the path you are walking along is beautiful and attractive enough. Come

Hamyangmun Gate and zelkova tree appearing in the *Painting of the Eastern Palaces*

Centuries-year-old zelkova tree seen from the wall surrounding Gwanmulheon Hall

on, how about sauntering along this shortcut, looking around here and there?

You see a zelkova tree boasting of its old age inside the wall when facing toward Gwanmulheon Hall at the starting point. The tree is now hundreds years old and it allowed palace painters to portray its looks in the *Painting of the Eastern Palaces*. As the route goes uphill, you will find the Queen's quarters called Daejojeon Hall over the wall on your left. You are already deep in the shade of trees, which exude sweet scents of the grove. You hear birds chirping from somewhere. In autumn, the maple tunnel ablaze with fiery red foliage presents a grand sight to behold.

The Rear Garden of Changdeokgung was a royal retreat and typical back yard of the Joseon Dynasty, which tried to make the best use of the natural beauty by building the garden on the hillside. The woods of the palace was called the 'Rear Garden', the 'Northern Garden', the 'Forbidden Garden', or the 'Royal Grove'. It is seated in the rear section of the palace precincts, hence the name of the 'Rear Garden.' Also, it is located in the northern section and it is not allowed to enter without permission, which gave birth to the names 'Northern Garden' and the 'Forbidden Garden'. The *Donggukyeojibigo* (東國輿地備考: Comparative review of anthropogeography around old Seoul, Hanyang) called the garden the 'Royal Grove.' And the office taking care of the gardens on the palace compound was named the 'Office of Royal Grove.'

The garden was not just a retreat. It was much more than for just taking a rest. Right here Joseon kings would pursue knowledge, discipline themselves, and ramble through the woods of the garden. It furnishes some buildings amid the lush woodland to allow the king some leeway away from extremely stressful kingship, enjoying hunting, practicing martial arts, hosting parties and offering sacrifices on the altar.

It was King Sejo, the seventh king of the dynasty, who expanded the scope of the Rear Garden to what it is now. According to *King Sejo's Annals*, the king ordered the rear garden to be enlarged because it was too humble and small. Seventy-three houses located in the residential district adjacent to the east of the garden were removed and the eastern section of the garden was expanded. The government had these residents moved out to any unoccupied lot they wanted. Then the next year, in the 9th year of King Sejo's reign, an additional 58 houses in the northern section of the garden was taken down. To the north the garden became closely bordered with the National Confucian Academy and to the east the fence was newly erected. It was around 1636, during King Injo's reign, that a large number of pavilions were built in the Rear Garden. The majority of pavilions remaining in the garden until now were made back then.

The Rear Garden now covers 300,000m^2 (74 acres), occupying roughly two-thirds of the gross area of the palace (480,000m^2, 118 acres). There are more than 160 species of trees growing there, and the number of trees older than 300 years is over 70. In addition, there are some 68 kinds of rare birds inhabiting the garden, which has made itself an ecological treasure house attracting academic attention.

Spring has come in the trail leading to the Rear Garden

The trail leading to the Rear Garden in summer

250

Autumnal view in the path leading to the Rear Garden

Snow-covered trail leading to the Rear Garden

251

Places to Be Seen Only with Mind's Eye

The Rear Garden does not allow you to appreciate the whole at just one glance, revealing its other looks whenever you run into different hills and valleys. Its diversity is revealed little by little only when you are deep inside nature. This is not the sight you just see, but the feasible substance you can grasp only when you are willing to breathe with nature and feel with your heart. Just take your time rambling around at a slow pace, and you will capture the very essence of the garden: small ponds, their pavilions chirping birds, murmuring brooks, the sky above, and trees all around them. Joseon kings would visit the rear garden with their officials to relieve the stress from state affairs, appreciating nature, improvising poems, and interacting with each other. They enjoyed riding horses through the woods, trained themselves through hunting, and competed with one another in shooting arrows. As you can imagine, the Rear Garden was not just a place for taking a rest, but a venue for holding important state occasions. Among others, military drills and state examinations were held at the Chundangdae Yard, and some royal events were performed to encourage the people in farming and weaving.

The pathway to the Rear Garden is aflame with autumnal tints.

11

Buyongjeong Pavilion

Dipped in Greenery

Buyongjeong Pavilion in the shape of a dainty lotus flower

Buyongjeong Pavilion and Buyongji Pond

The shaded pathway ends and there the road slopes down to a scenic spot which opens out onto a picturesque view. But there is no big hurry. You do not need to rush to the foot of the hill. It might be better to overlook from a distance your next destination, The Gujanggak Royal Library. The two-story building standing on top of steep stairs is the Gujanggak Royal Library, and the single story structure with a large yard is Yeonghwadang

Buyongji Pond and its vicinity overlooked from the downhill road

Buyongjeong Pavilion

Pavilion. Then go a little further downward, you will see a pavilion dipping its feet in a big square pond. This ornate pavilion is called Buyongjeong or Lotus Pavilion. Now you have got to the Rear Garden of Changdeokgung Palace at last.

Here in the Gyujanggak Library area is the Buyongjeong Pavilion bashfully perched on the southern bank of the pond. In the 33rd year of King Sukjong's rule (1707), they dug a pond where the wells had been located during King Sejo's reign and built a house called Taeksujae by the pond. Then the pond was remade, the house was rebuilt, and it was renamed Buyongjeong Pavilion in 1792 when King Jeongjo ascended the throne.

258

Buyongji Pond, a square pond with a round islet at the center, represents a fairyland of immortal beings in Taoist tradition

'Buyong' literally means lotus flower. As the name stands for, the cross-shaped pavilion is in the shape of pure lotus flower which is about to blossom. The stylish pavilion is surrounded by decorative balustrades on all sides, with the northern projected section elevated to mark a royal seat. If you take the royal seat with windows open, you may feel like you are riding a boat floating on the water, or you may even imagine you are now doing footbath on a hot summer day, immersing your feet into the cool water.

Buyongji Pond, an artificial pond with a man-made round

The summer has come to Buyongjeong Pavilion

islet, is patterned after a Taoist idea that heaven is round and the earth square (天圓地方). The idea means the virtue of heaven lies in being round and smooth, and that of the earth lies in straight and even. The islet in the middle has a pine tree belonging to the fairyland, which is a metaphor that you have got to the pond and now become an immortal being residing in the fairyland. The *Painting of the Eastern Palaces* (東闕圖) portrays the pond with two boats floating in. King Jeongjo had a great time fishing at the pond. Whenever the king hooked a fish, music was played to add to the fun and the fish was released back into the pond.

To the west of the pond stands a small tablet house. It is

Next to the stele shed, there is a water inlet decorated with a pattern of a monster serpent and wild plum flowers

called Stele Shed of Four Wells or Sajeonggibigak (四井記碑閣) and tells you a history of the Buyongji vicinity. During King Sejo's reign, the king ordered Prince Yeongsun and Prince Osan to look for some wells and they located four sites of wells, two sites each. Those wells were named Mani (摩尼), Paryeo (玻瓈), Yuri (琉璃), and Okjeong (玉井). But over a long period of time they went through a couple of fires of

261

Two wells were recently restored at their original locations.

war and ended up only two wells being left with no other trace. Moreover, the neighborhood was overgrown with weeds and looked bleak and desolate. Then in the 16th year of King Sukjong's reign, they got the two remaining wells repaired and the Stele of four wells erected with engravings on the whole story. To the north of the stele shed, you can find two sites of wells that were recently restored.

One lovely summer day, a long-necked heron has come to look
around the Buyongji Pond.

Eosumun Gate and Juhamnu Pavilion seen through
the snow-covered branches of winter trees

Eosumun Gate and Green Fence, *Chwibyeong*

The main gate leading up to the Juhamnu Pavilion perched on the hilly ground is named Eoseonmun Gate. 'Eeosu (魚水)' whose literal translation is fish and water came from a Chinese legend; ✿Sueojigyo (水魚之交) means a firm and intimate friendship like that of Damon and Pythias in ancient Greece. 'Eo (魚)' of Eosumun points to King's subjects and 'su (水)' indicates King Jeongjo himself. 'Eosumun' signifies King's subjects should revolve around King's political leadership just as fish cannot live without water. King Jeongjo laid great emphasis on the King's active role in the political arena. The gate name of Eosumun

> ✿ Sueojigyo : a Chinese legend introduced in the *Records of the Three Kingdoms* (三國志) means a firm and intimate friendship like that of Damon and Pythias in ancient Greece. Liu Bei (劉備: founded the state of Shu Han (蜀漢) in the Three Kingdoms (三國) period) became very close to Zhuge Liang (諸葛亮) and often had discussions with him. Guan Yu (關羽) and Zhang Fei (張飛) were not pleased and complained. Liu Bei explained, "Now that I have Kongming (Zhuge Liang's style name), I am like a fish that has found water. I hope you will stop making unpleasant remarks." Guan Yu and Zhang Fei then stopped complaining.

Eosumun Gate. The overhead beam of the gate is crested with intertwined dragons in brattishing.

reveals not only King Jeongjo's strong will to advocate open selection of talented officials but also his confidence to control them with authority as an omnipotent monarch.

Staircases to Juhamnu Pavilion have three narrow gates. The one in the center is quite bigger and has exquisite window dressing as the main gate of the pavilion. The gate itself is not so big, but its decoration is so huge that it assumes dignified appearances: the name plaque of Eosumun hung vertically, the overhead beam crested with intertwined dragons, and the stone balustrades ornamented with cloud. The gate was reserved for

266

Arabesque pattern on the pillars and cloud design on the stone banisters

the king only and his officials had to pass through the small, low gates on both sides. King Jeongjo made every effort to call in the best brains. Also, the king made sure that his competent staff should behave with modesty by making them bend their back down in order to pass through the low gates.

There are hedges made of bamboo stalks to the sides of the Eosumun. They are called *Chwibyeong* (翠屛: quickset screens with bamboo frames). The *Painting of the Eastern Palaces* (東闕圖) shows living hedges were planted on several sections of the palace. '*Chwibyeong*' is literally translated as 'green screen fence.' It is a traditional hedge enclosure that is less overbearing than stone or brick walls, but has enough marking-out effect by using live hedge instead of hard materials like stones or bricks. It helps feel nature-friendly as well as partitions the space visually.

Chibyeong installed on both sides of the Eosumun Gate makes
the Juhamnu section neat and snug.

King Jeongjo's Dream Centered
at Gyujanggak Library and Juhamnu Pavilion

To the north of the Buyongjeong Pavilion is a two-story structure seated on top of steep stairs. Its name plaque reads ✿ Juhamnu (宙合樓). In 1776 when King Jeongjo ascended the throne, he built the two-story building and named the lower floor Gyujanggak (奎章閣), the Royal Archives, and the upper floor Juhamnu, its reading room. 'Juhamnu' means a place which is opening onto the universe. 'Juhap (宙合)' out of Juhamnu (宙合樓) denotes that six entities get united (六合) and six entities are

The first floor is Gyujanggak Library, and the second floor Juhamnu Pavilion

269

Balusters of Juhamnu Pavilion

heaven, earth, and four directions, south, east and west- that is
to say the universe. 'Gyujang (奎章)' means royal handwritings and
texts. Gujanggak Library represents the place Gyusu (奎宿), the
constellation in charge of literary works, is illuminating.

> ✿ Juhamnu : The word of Juhamnu consists of Juhap (宙合) and ru (樓).
> However, when Juhap and ru are combined, they are pronounced as
> Juhamnu, not as Juhapru, due to phonetic rule of Korean.

Cloud-patterned banister of the stairway leading to Gyujanggak Hall

During King Jeongjo's reign, Gyujanggak served as the think tank that churned out policies supporting political reforms driven by the king. Initially Gyujanggak was started by King Sukjong as a division belonging to *Jongbusi* (宗薄寺: Royal Pedigree Office). It was set up to have royal clansmen keep kings' texts and handwritings in place. King Jeongjo was enthroned at Gyeonghuigung Palace in March, 1776. Around three months later, he ordered the construction of a new Gyujanggak, the Royal Archives, in the Rear Garden of Changdeokgung Palace and had it completed in September. In addition, to the southwest he erected Bongmodang (奉謨堂) Hall enshrining the kings' portraits and royal records. To the due south he also built a two-story building, Yeolgogwan (閱古觀) to store stacking domestically published books, and next to it Gaeyuwa (皆有窩) keeping books published overseas. To the west was made a facility called Seohyanggak (書香閣) to give an airing to books on a regular basis, and several annex buildings were added including another book storage to the northwest.

King Jeongjo transformed the small book storage Gyujanggak

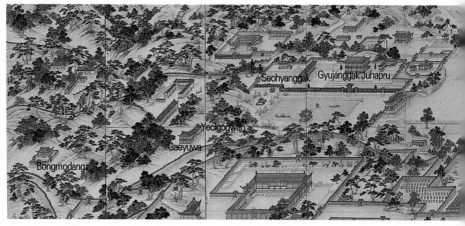

The *Painting of Eastern Palace* shows Gyujanggak and its vicinity.

into a royal library Gyujanggak. The small storage just storins royal texts, royal clan genealogy and other supplies was transformed into a royal library housing so many valuable books published at home and abroad. Then Gyujanggak Royal Library was transfigured into a think tank where young, competent staff of officials engaged themselves in research. As these officials got experienced and their roles expanded, the term *Gyujanggak* referred to the advisory body for the king encompassing all the core functions as secretariat, policy maker, and publisher. King Jeongjo is acclaimed to have initiated the renaissance during the latter half of Joseon. Gyujanggak Royal Library was the very cradle of the renaissance.

The Gateway to Success:
Legend of a Carp Leaping over Dragon Gate

On the southern corner of the Buyongjeong Pond, the large stone block at the top has a carving of carp which is about to be soaring up into the air. The fish has its origin in an old story of 'fish turned into dragon.' The old story says that a school of carp got together every year to jump up against the swift current at the gorge of the Dragon Gate (龍門) in the upper Yellow River

Buyongjeong Pavilion seen from the southern corner of the pond

(黃河) in China, and that only a few of them that could leap up over the rapids were able to turn into a dragon. That made the legend of a carp leaping over the Dragon Gate (登龍門), which means the gateway to success in life.

Carp in embossed carving

'Leaping over the Dragon Gate (登龍門)' is actually better known to Koreans as the name of a famous cram school for university entrance. Then, could it be just a coincidence that the gate leading to Gyujanggak is named Eosumun (fish and water gate).

The Gyujanggak vicinity alludes to the tale of a *seonbi* (traditional Confucian scholar) that absorbed himself in academic research to pass the tough state examinations, started a career in government to make his way in the world, got promoted in rank to take up the prime minister's position, and finally achieved fame and prestige. But his life story is not complete without finding a missing piece of the whole picture. Spotting the missing part is the very charm of rambling around the Rear Garden. To the east of the Gyujanggak Hall, you find a building with spacious grounds and the building is called Yeonghwadang Pavilion.

Yeonghwadang Pavilion seen from the back of Buyongjeong Pavilion

Here you have a good view of Yeonghwadang Pavilion
and Chundangdae Field.

Yeonghwadang Pavilion and Chundangdae Field

Yonghwadang Pavilion stands to the southeast of the Gyujanggak Hall, and its front yard is called Chundangdae Field. Currently a big wall is lying in front of the pavilion, separating the precincts of Chandeokgung and Changgyeonggung Palace. But it was not like this back then. Originally it was an ample ground with no wall in between, where royal guards staged their military drills and the king inspected their field exercises under

Yeonghwadang Pavilion

277

command.

Chundangdae was the venue for important state events. Among others, the final round of state examinations called *Jeonsi* (殿試: court exam) was held in the presence of the king. You cannot make complete the legend of a carp leaping over the Dragon Gate without referring to the state exams. The national tests were sometimes administered at the Chundangdae Field with the king being seated at the pavilion and observing all the *seonbis* in person. King Jeongjo wrote a poem about the scenic view of the candidates taking a test: *Yeonghwasisa* (暎花試士: *seonbis* putting their abilities to the test in front of Yeonghwadang Pavilion). The poem is one of the 10 quadrains with seven-letter lines whose theme are the *Sangrim Sipgyeong* (上林十景: ✿Ten scenic views of the Royal Grove). They

✿ Ten Scenic Views of the Royal Grove

1. Plowing at Gwanpunggak Pavilion in spring (觀豐春景)
2. Cuckoo chirping at Mangchunjeong Pavilion (望春聞鶯)
3. Late spring at Cheonhyanggak Pavilion (天香春晚)
4. Boat riding in front of Eosudang Hall (魚水泛舟)
5. Floating wine cups at Soyoam Rock (逍遙流觴)
6. Appreciating lotus flowers at Huiujeong Pavilion (喜雨賞蓮)
7. Moon on a clear day at Cheongsimjeong (清心霽月)
8. Autumn foliage at Gwandeokjeong Pavilion (觀德楓林)
9. *Seoubis* taking a test in front of Younghwadang Pavilion (暎花試士)
10. Snowing in the evening at Neungheojeong Pavilion (凌虛暮雪)

278

Yeonghwadang Pavilion and its Stone Platform

are included in *Hongjaejeonseo* (弘齋全書: King Jeongjo's anthology). Shall we appreciate ten beautiful views of the Rear Garden just like King Jeongjo did?

Also, it is at this Yeonghwadang you can welcome another dramatic hero of the past. Yi Mongryong, the main character of *Chunhyangjeon* (春香傳: The story of Chunhyang), took a state exam in the Chundangdae Field. The *Chunhyangjeon* is one of the best known love stories and folk tales of Korea. The story says Yi Mongryong won the first place in a state examination held here at the Chundangdae and was appointed as a secret royal inspector, who would investigate and prosecute corrupt government officials as an undercover emissary of the king. Under disguise, he came to Chunhyang's village and found out what had happened to Chunhyang, his first love and wife, and how wickedly the new magistrate had treated her.

Sundial installed in front of the Yeonghwadang Pavilion

The story starts out like this: One day Yi Mongryong, who was a son of a local governor and always studied hard, went out to get some fresh air. He saw Chunhyang on a swing and fell in love with her at the first sight. She was a daughter of Wolmae, a retired *gisaeng* (Korean geisha). He ordered his servant Bangja to ask Chunhyang to come to him, but she refused. Yi Mongryong went to talk to Chunhyang's mother Wolmae to ask for permission to marry Chunhyang; Wolmae gave her permission to him and the two young people got married that day.

Then Yi Mongryong's father, a government official, was transferred to another region, Hanyang (current Seoul), so Yi Mongryong had to leave Chunhyang to follow his father. After he left, a new magistrate came to Chunhyang's village. The new governor was so greedy and wicked. He always wasted his time at partying with *gisaengs*. Chunhyang, renowned for her beauty, was forced to come to his party. Although Chunhyang was not a

280

gisaeng, the governor treated her like one because her mother had been on the *gisaeng* roster. So he compelled her to sleep with him, but Chunhyang kept refusing him because she was a married woman. The governor got angry and imprisoned her. He decided to punish Chunhyang on his birthday.

The story goes on as follows: Even if Mongryong figured out the situation, he had to conceal his real identity, so he acted like an insane person in mendicant clothes. Despite his beggarly appearance, Chunhyang still loved him and asked her mother to take good care of him. At the magistrate's birthday celebration, Yi Mongryong came in and made a satirical poem about the misbehavior of the governor, but he did not understand the poem. Yi Mongryong disclosed his real position and punished the governor. At first, Chunhyang could not recognize Yi Mongryong when he tested her faith by asking her to spend a night with him. Chunhyang, unable to recognize him, refused him as well. However, she soon realized who he was and they lived happily ever after.

The state examination at the Chundangdae was one of the special exams irregularly held, but acted as good as the court examination taking place in the presence of the king. It was irregularly offered to celebrate joyous events for royal family or put confucianists' capacity to the test. It was initiated by King Seonjo in 1572 to select civil servants and military officers. The king visited in person to the test site of Chundangdae located in the Rear Garden. The Chundangdae Exam had the same merit as passing the last phase of the three-stage higher level court examination called *daegwa*. According to the *Chunhyangjeon*, Yi Mongryong passed the national test as the first place winner at his first attempt after only one-year-long preparation. His dramatic success was just an exaggeration for fun of the fiction. However, passing the Chundangdae exam must have served as 'Leaping over the Dragon Gate(登龍門)' for all the ambitious Confucian literati that dreamed of winning the first place at the state exams.

Seated on Yeonghwadang Pavilion, waiting for spring to come to the Buyongji Pond.

Spring view of Buyongji Pond seen from Yeonghwadang Pavilion

Seohyanggak Hall, Huiujeong Pavilion, and Jewolgwangpunggwan Hall

To the west of the Gyujanggak Library stands the Seohyanggak Hall. The hall once served as a royal portrait hall where kings' portraits were enshrined. Sometimes it was used to store books or give books an airing, The front of the hall has a vertical sign board on the pillar reading Eochianjamsil (御親蠶室: Royal silkworm-raising room) and another hanging board reading

Seohyanggak Hall and its sign boards

Chinjamgwonmin (親蠶勸民: Encouraging people to raise silkworms) over the door. According to records, the queen gave demonstrations on feeding silkworms in 1777 (the first year of King Jeongjo's reign) and during Japanese rule. That demonstration called *Chinjamnye* (親蠶禮: In-person Sericulture ceremony) was a national ceremony presided over by the queen, as the 'state mother', to experience women's labor in person and promote sericulture. The queen was accompanied by an entourage of noble ladies to conduct ceremonial harvesting of mulberry leaves for feeding the silkworms. That is why many mulberry trees are planted on the palace grounds. One of them is the 400-year-old mulberry tree on the right section around the Aeryeonji Pond. That tree is protected as a Natural Monument. Also, there used to be rice paddies cultivated by the royal court, so that the king could experience his people's labor and encourage farming by demonstrating the work himself. Those royal rice paddies were located next to the Chundangdae field in front of the Yeonghwadang Hall according to the *Painting of the Eastern Palaces*.

On the hill over Seohyanggak lies a small and humble pavilion called Huiujeong, which is ont painted with *dancheong*. 'Huiu' means 'happy rainfall.' The pavilion built in the early 17th century was initially called 'Chuihyangjeong' and had a straw-thatched roof. In 1690, the 16th year of King Sukjong's reign, drought lasted all summer and the king sent his minister to the pavilion to hold a ritual for rain. The ritual at the pavilion worked and they got a satisfying amount of rainfall. The king was so pleased with the result that he changed the roof from a straw-thatched one to a roof-tiled one and renamed the pavilion Huiujeong. Huiujeong provides a wonderful view overlooking lotus flowers on the Buyongji Pond and the view is one of the Ten scenic views of the Royal Grove (上林十景); 'Appreciating lotus flowers at Huiujeong pavilion (喜雨相蓮).' Surrounded by snug little fences to the west, the pavilion retains admirable beauty all year round.

On the hill northeast of Juhamnu stands a building called Cheonseokjeong Hall. It lies on the same height with the Huiujeong

Huiujeong Pavilion

Jewolgwangpunggwan Pavilion

Pavilion. The hall has the name plaque, Jewolgwangpunggwan (霽月光風觀), which belongs to the pavilion attached to the hall. According to the book named *Donggukyeojibigo*, "Cheonseokjeong is located east of Juhamnu and it has a small pavilion whose signboard reads Jewolgwangpungnu (霽月光風樓)." 'Jewolgwangpung' means 'bright moonlight and fresh breeze after the rain', and it is more commonly known as Gwangpung-jewol. As the suffix '*gwan* (觀)' or '*nugwan* (樓觀)' means a pavilion, Jewolgwangpungnu signifies a pavilion standing on the spot that commands a wonderful view.

287

Snow-covered Seohyanggak Hall and Gyujanggak Library

Snow-covered Huiujeong Pavilion

12

Aeryeonjeong Pavilion
Tinged with Autumnal Hues

When autumn is in full swing with leaves of crimson and orange shades,
Aeryeonji Pond is enchantingly beautiful.

Bullomun Gate and Aeryeonjeong Pavilion

Bullomun (不老門) Gate is a stone gate standing abreast of Geummamun (金馬門) Gate. 'Bullo' means never-getting-old. The gate is made of stone, one of the Ten Longevity symbols, and imbued with Taoist ideology. It gives blessing of eternal youth to anybody who passes through the gate. Carved out of a monolith, the gate is erected in the vicinity of Aeryeonji Pond.

Bullomun Gate and Aeryeonjeong Pavilion

Bullomun is a gate carved out of a monolith.

Autumn has come to Aeryeonjeong Pavilion.

Passing through Bullomun, you find Aeryeonjeong Pavilion (愛
蓮亭) on the northern end of the pond on the way up to
Yeongyeongdang Hall. 'Aeryeon' means love for lotuses. Zhou
Dunyi (周敦頣), a Neo-Confucian philosopher of Song China, wrote
a buzzed-about poem called '*Aeryeonseol* (愛蓮說)'.

According to *Gunggwolji* (宮闕志: Book of palaces), King Sukjong
set up an islet topped by a pavilion in the middle of the pond
and named the pavilion 'Aeryeonjeong'. The *Aeryeonjeonggi* (愛蓮
亭記: The Record of Aeryeonjeong) written by King Sukjong said the
pavilion was erected in the center of the pond, but the current
Aeryeonjeong is standing on the northern end, which means it

Uiduhap Hall seen through the pillars of Aeryeonjeong Pavilion

was rebuilt later. Two out of four pavilion legs are dipping into the pond, and half of the structure is above the water and the other half remains on the embankment. When you see a small house on the opposite side called Gioheon Study from Aeryeonjeong, the scenery looks like a painting in the frame. By adorning the doorposts and lintel of the pavilion with elaborately painted wooden panels, a big picture frame is created and the view of the other side turns into a vivid painting.

296

Zelkova tree in front of Aeryeonji Pond has changed
into an autumn outfit.

Water is drawn into the pond through the headrace carved on the big flagstone, which adds to the picturesque beauty. The northwest stylobate of the pond is engraved with Taeaek (太液). 'Taeaek' means a huge amount of water. These days a pond is generally named after its pavilion like Aeryeonji Pond came from Aeryeonjeong Pavilion and Buyongji Pond from Buyongjeong Pavilion, but back then any pond, a pool of water, seemed to be just called Taeaek.

Through the head race carved on the flagstone, water is drawn into the pond.

'Taeaek' engraving on the northwest stylobate of the pond

The flagstone of Aeryeonji Pond

298

Pond next to Eosudang Site

There are another pond and a vacant lot to the west of Aeryeonji. The vacant ground used to be occupied by Eosudang Hall. The hall has disappeared, but the pond remains. In autumn the Aeryeojeong and Yeongyeongdang vicinities dress up in red and yellow tints. Just imagine yourself under the bright moonlight, sitting on the Aeryeonjeong Pavilion and listening to a *daegeum* (a transverse bamboo flute) melody.

Even in bleak and desolate winter, Aeryeonjeong is beautiful.

Winter foliage of Aeryeonnjeong stands out vividly
against the snow.

Uiduhap Hall of Crown Prince Hyomyeong

It is said that there was Geummamun (金馬門) Gate in Mianggung Palace (未央宮) of Han China with a bronze horse standing next to it. Also, 'Geumma' is the name of the national archive during the Han Dynasty. Passing through the gate, you find the Gihoheon Study of Crown Prince Hyomyeong (1807~1830). It seems that Geummamun Gate was named following the Han

Geummamun Gate

302

Gihoheon Study

Chinese tradition since the study was stacked with lots of books.

The *Gunggwolji* (Book of Palaces) said Uiduhap (倚斗閣) Hall seated north of the Yeonghwadang Pavilion was a study room. 'Uidu (倚斗)' means depending upon the Big Dipper. The Big dipper pointed to King Jeongjo, Crown Prince Hyomyeong's grandfather, since the king was admired as his role model. Actually, Uiduhap is standing right behind the Gyujanggak Library. He seems to have made his intention clear by selecting the site for Uiduhap as leaning against the Gyujanggak, which was his grandfather's think tank. The prince was poised to solidify royal authority, to break down dominating in-law families, and to make his political

Uiduhap Hall seen from Aereonji Pond

visions come true.

Crown Prince Hyomyeong, the first son of King Sunjo, had such wonderful character, special talent and admirable ability that he was admired as brilliant gentleman and took office as the prince regent from the age of 19. Unfortunately, though, he passed away at 22. He was posthumously given the title of King Ikjong after his son ascended the throne. During his regency, he established ceremonial music and dance of the Joseon Dynasty to uphold royal dignity and tradition. It was Crown Prince Hyomyeong who created a court dance called Chunaengjeon Dance (春鶯轉: solo dance performed in yellow dress as a symbol of an oriole).

What pretty steps you are taking under the moonlight!

Your silk sleeves waving in the wind do look as if they are dancing.

Also, the crown prince revived the choreography of the ancient Goguryeo and Silla kingdoms. As for ceremonial music and dance of Korea, he is regarded as second only to King Sejong the Great. Moreover, he is thought to have taken the initiative in producing the '*Picture of the Eastern Palaces* (東闕圖)'

Name plaque of Gioheon Study

Ungyeonggeo Storage, the smallest structure in the palace precincts

as the prince regent. That is because its estimated production date (1824~1830) concurred with his regency. Although he secured such a virtue and intelligence, he could not ascend the throne. Only after he passed away, he could assume the posthumous title of king. However, his three-year-regency was meaningful enough to make Joseon society pin hopes on a new era. It seemed that the blossom was gone too early, but its fragrance remained strong enough to make anybody look back on his legacy.

Currently, the hall has a sign

Embankments at the back of Gioheon bearing engravings of Choyeondae and Chuseongdae

board reading Gioheon (寄傲軒), which points to the open wooden floor of Uiduhap. 'Gio (寄傲)' means depending on your pride. The name of Gioheon came from a phrase of *Returning to the Fields* (歸去來辭: *Gui Qu Lai Ci*) written by Tao Yuanming (陶淵明, 365~427), a Chinese poet during the Six Dynasties period. He said, "Now I am leaning against the southern window to depend on my pride. I feel so cozy however cramped my room is (倚南窓以寄傲 審容膝之以安)." It is obvious that 'Gio' and 'Uidu' have their pride in common. His grandfather, King Jeongjo was his pride and Crown Prince underscored he was depending on his grandfather and leaning on him for support. Also, to the west of Uiduhap lies a small building called Ungyeonggeo Storage. It is an annex to the Uiduhap Hall.

Steep slopes behind the Gioheon have many-layered embankments and a series of stairs leading up to the Gyujanggak Library. Two stone blocks of these embankments have engravings of Choyeondae (超然臺) and Chuseongdae (秋聲臺). 'Choyeon' means keeping calm and aloof.

Laozi (老子) said, 'Even if you are allowed to lead a sumptuous life, you try to keep calm and aloof.' Chuseong (秋聲) means all the sounds in autumn including sounds of winds, insects fallen leaves. Placed abreast with Choyeondae, Chuseongdae signifies the voices from Mother Nature in the midst of the bountiful autumn scene. Prince Hyomyeong composed *Ten Scenic Views of Uiduhap* to express the beauty of its vicinity.

Stairs and a gate leading up to the Gyujanggak Library
from the Uiduhap Hall.

A small door on the southern wall of Ungyeonggeo Storage
topped with autumnal colors

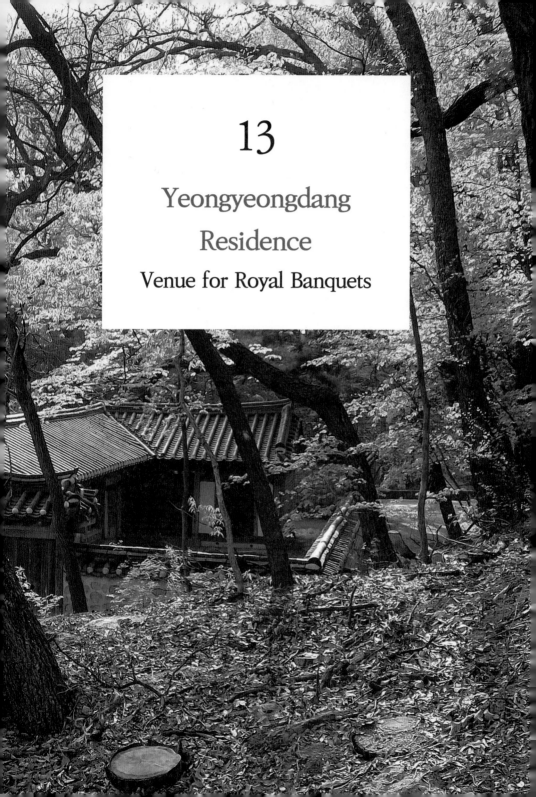

13

Yeongyeongdang
Residence

Venue for Royal Banquets

Fall has come to the doorsteps of Yeongyeongdang Residence.

Fairy-tale hermits live in Yeongyeongdang Residence

Yeongyeongdang (演慶堂) Residence was dedicated to King Sunjo by his son, Crown Prince Hyomyeong, to celebrate his 40th birthday. The residence was built in 1828 as a venue for royal ceremonies and events. 'Yeongyeong (演慶)' means extending congratulations. In November of the 28th year of King Sunjo's reign, the prince petitioned the king to let him make celebration

Jangnakmun Gate

Waterway flowing under the western wall of Yeongyeongdang finds its way into Eosudang Site.

plans for his father's 40th birthday. As soon as he was granted permission, he began to organize the event by setting up the banquetsite. The celebration meant a lot as the occasion marking not only King Sunjo's 40th birthday, but also the 30th anniversary of his accession to the throne.

Yeongyeongdang has a tall gate as its main gate, and the name plaque of Jangnakmun (長樂門) is hung on the façade of its gate. The main gates of Yeongyeongdang Hall and Nakseonjae Residence share the same name of Jangnakmun. In front of the main gate there is an oddly shaped rock planted in a big stone pot. The stone pot has four small toad carvings on each corner

Oddly-shaped rock in front of Jangnakmun Gate

Toad carving on the corner of the stone pot

A relief of the dog on the stone pot before
Yeongyeongdang Residence

of its rim. The Toad is a symbol of Chinese goddess of the Moon, Hang-a (姮娥: Chang'e) and suggests that Yeongyeongdang is a fairyland where fairy-tale hermits are living.

Turning your eyes to your feet, you find a waterway running under the western wall of Yeongyeongdang that flows through the front of the main gate, and into the pond of Eosudang Site. The wall does not block water flowing, so the water comes inside the wall a little bit and then runs out. Joseon people tried not to obstruct water's way when erecting their buildings. Nature could keep its firm but calm stance.

In order to get into Jangnakmun, you need to cross a stream before the gate. People call the stream 'the Milky Way (銀

315

Passing through Jangnakmun Gate, you find servants' quarters, storage and a stable.

河水: literally, the Silvery River)' and the bridge over the stream 'Crow and magpie bridge (烏鵲橋).' All are intended to suggest Yeongyeongdang belongs to the fairyland.

The meeting of the two love-stars: According to mythology, Altair and Vega in the sky can meet only once a year on the night of July 7 by the lunar calendar, when crows and magpies work together to form a bridge squeezing their bodies together between the two love-stars. People say crows and magpies do not have feathers on their head after the day, since the two lovers stepped on their heads.

Yeongyeongdang has no *dancheong* (丹青: traditional multicolored

Suinmun Gate on the left is for women and Jangyangmun Gate on the right for men.

paintwork) and looks like a nobleman's residence, not palace buildings. It was constructed to give the king a firsthand experience of nobility's life. It was patterned after the conventional 99-square kan residence of a nobleman, but it has a bigger 120-square *kan* scale (*kan*: a Korean measurement unit meaning the distance between two pillars, or the square area made up of four pillars).

King Sunjo is said to have stayed at Yeongyeongdang Residence dressed in plain clothes just like ordinary literati-scholars. Actually, the residence provided a shelter to King Sunjo who was really fed up with the in-law families' dominance over state affairs. Afterwards, King Gojong and the Enlightment Party

317

members sought refuge here from Qing Chinese troops during the Gapsin coup in 1884. Then it served for political needs like receiving foreign diplomats and holding parties. Also, Emperor Sunjong and his empress took it up as their quarters when a fire destroyed their residences in 1917.

Passing through Jangnakmun, you find servants' quarters, storage, a stable, and toilets on your right and left. Inside the main gate there are two middle gates; Jangyangmun Gate to men's quarters to the east and Suinmun Gate to women's ones to the west. Jangyangmun is a tall gate and higher than Suinmun. All gate means a gate that is raised high above the roof of the servants' quarters so as to let a mono-wheeled sedan chair for high ranking officials pass through. Suinmun is a plain gate and

Lantern pedestal

has a tree before it. Back then people planted trees aside from the center of the front yard. The tree in the compound is called *jeongsimsu* (正心樹), which means an arbor that helps keep right-minded. If you planted a tree (木) in the center of the precincts, that would make a similar image to 困 (exhausted) or 閑 (idle) and have unlucky and ominous implications. Due to this reason, it looks like they avoided planting trees in the center. In practice, planting trees in the center of the house is not so good. It is a time-honored custom not to have inside the compound a tall tree which would cast much shadow over the building. There are two stone pedestals set up before Jangyangmun. They are stands for lighting where pine twigs were burned or lanterns were placed.

Passing through Jangyangmun Gate, you will be in the front yard of Yeongyeongdang Residence bordered with *naeoedam* wall.

Sarangchae Quarters and *Naeoedam* Wall

Yeongyeongdang was originally the name of *sarangchae* quarters (men's quarters), but it can also indicate the whole complex like Yeongyeongdang Residence, or Yeongyeongdang Quarters. *Sarangchae* has an open wooden-floored hall in the middle, and a reception room and a loft on both sides. The reception room was a host's chamber where the host would receive visitors, have

Yeongyeongdang Quarters

Open wooden-floored hall of Yeongyeongdang Quarters

a friendly talk, or discuss current issues with his friends and colleagues, that is to say, a parlor for socializing with other gentlemen.

Name plaque of Yeongyeongdang

To the west of the front yard, a low brick wall called *naeoedam* wall divides *sarangchae* from *anchae* quarters (women's quarters). However, the wall is so low that you can look over the women's area if you stand on tiptoe. Confucian teaching of Joseon sternly required dividing the space for men and women, thus needing the wall, but such a low *naeoedam* wall looks quite winsome and amiable, rather than strict. At the end of the wall between the men's and women's quarters, you find a wicket door. Peeking through the wicket door, they could count the number of visitors from the number of shoes and prepare tea or food for them accordingly. You can also see a horse block placed in front of the *sarangchae* for men to step on when they dismounted from a horse.

Wicket door

The *Anchae* quarters located to the right of the *sarangchae* is the space for the hostess. Men's and women's quarters look separate because they have the wall in between, but their insides are connected in a straight line. Stand on the west end of *anchae* and look through the open doors, and you will notice how beautiful the inner structure is. The northern wall of the women's section includes the Tongbyeokmun Gate. Behind the gate there are additional quarters for household chores, which are called *banbitgan* quarters. *Banbitgan* consists of a kitchen, storage, a wooden-floored hall, and an *ondol* room (equipped with heating system). Here did housemaids their jobs such as cooking, sewing, and doing laundry.

322

Naeoedam wall seen from the women's quarters

The interior of Yeongyeongdang Quarters is connected in a straight line.

Insides of both quarters are linked with each other.

A chimney and winter grove seen through a door of the Yeongyeongdang Residence

Suinmun Gate leads you to the *anchae* of
Yeongyeongdang Residence.

Anchae quarters dyed with autumn colors

Anchae quarters on a snowy day

327

The last leaves over the snow-covered roof of *Banbitgan* quarters

Tongbyeokmun Gate and *banbitgan* seen from *anchae* quarters

Tongbyeokmun Gate and *banbitgan*

329

Seonhyangjae Study and
Nongsujeong Pavilion

The western corridor building of Yeongyeongdang Quarters is called Cheongsujeongsa (清水精舍) Retreat, which means the seat of learning with surrounding water. The retreat seems to have been a place where poets, artists, and calligraphers would stay.

Seonhyangjae (善香齋) Study to the west of the *sarangchae* was where the host would receive guests. Back in the Joseon Dynasty,

Cheongsujeongsa Retreat

330

The sunshade of the Seonhyangjae Study

influential officials got lots of visitors and guests frequenting their residences in and out of the season, so hosts needed guest rooms for letting them stay for days. 'Seonhyang (善香: good fragrance)' means fragrance from books. The study faces west and its wide eaves block the glaring afternoon sunlight. The sunshade is made of copper plates and its angle is adjusted with pulleys and hemp cords. The gable roof tile at the end of northern eaves has an engraving of *gam*-sign (坎 ☵) out of divination's eight trigrams from the *Book of Changes*. The *gam*-sign signifies water and you can find six *gam*-signs at the six corners of the roof. That means the building is completely soaked in water and it will never catch fire. Both sidewalls of the study are complete with monotonous red bricks. This type of final touch came from the architectural style of Qing China. The sidewalls are decorated with a flower pattern of *taepyeongwha* (太平花), which looks like a lotus

taepyeongwha

331

flower and has four or six petals adorned with grass leaves. It means the peaceful world and a symbol of the reign of undisturbed peace.

Nongsujeong (濃繡亭) Pavilion perches on the top tier of the stone terrace behind Seonhyangjae Study. 'Nongsu' means being embroidered in deep colors, and it gives a vivid description of the pavilion that is seated deep inside the Yeongyeongdang Quarters and shrouded in green shades all the time. Next to the pavilion is Taeilmun Gate leading you to the Rear Garden. Passing through the gate, you find a trail through the woods. Walking a little further along the trail takes you to another pavilion called Seungjaejeong.

Nongsujeong

Nongsujeong Pavilion seen from the hill near Taeilmun Gate

Let's take a break for a moment, sitting on the Seonhyangjae verandah
and listening to the sounds of the forest.

If you want to be a fairy-tale hermit, why not sign up for the 'Moonlight Tour at Changdeokgung Palace? Following the moonlight with a lantern, you will get to the Nakseonjae Complex. Now, cross the threshold of the full moon-shaped gate in its rear garden. The gate was created by Joseon people who yearned to embrace the full moon in their heart.

Then walk along the long trail to the Rear Garden, and you will get to Buyongjeong Pavilion and Gyujanggak Library. The bright moon is so shy that it is about to hide between clouds. Passing through Bullomun Gate and arriving at Yeongyeongdang Residence, you get soaked under the moonlight in a melody of Korean folk music, which is the blessing given only to those who visit Chandeokgung. The palace at night is a far cry from that during the daytime: the world serene and peaceful. Shall we take a stroll along the trail in the night, listening to scops owl tweeting, brook murmuring, breeze whispering, and our own footstep rustling? Trees cast their dim shadows over the corner of the eaves in a monotone. The clear tunes of the *daegeum* (the traverse bamboo flute) soars through the chilly night air up to the tree branches and the moonlight. Treading on the bright moonlight in the Rear Garden after a rain clear off, you may naturally share the poetic sentiment with King Jeongjo at last, as he recited 'Moon on a clear day at Cheongsimjeong (淸心霽月) from his series of poetry called *Ten Scenic Views of the Royal Grove.*

Silk lantern illuminating 'Moonlight Tour'

Passing through Taeilmun Gate, you find a trail to the Rear Garden.

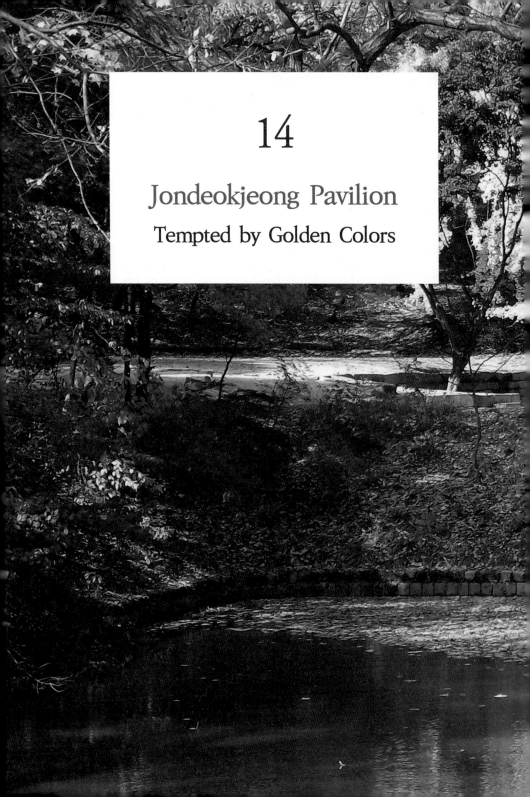

14

Jondeokjeong Pavilion
Tempted by Golden Colors

Northern pond reflecting lush greenery

Jondeokjeong Pavilion and Banweolji Pond

Shall we now leave for the more secluded interior of the Rear Garden? There are two paths leading you to Jondeokjeong (尊德亭) Pavilion: One is taking a shortcut from Aeryeonji Pond to the pavilion without passing through Bullomun Gate, and the other is passing through Taeilmun Gate of the Yeongyeongdang Residence. If you have enough time, the latter will suit you much

Jondeokjeong Pavilion in winter

Small stone bridge and stonework of Jondeokjeong Pavilion

better since the trail is so picturesque. The small hill outside
Taeilmun enables you to look back at Yeongyeongdang. The
angle looking backward on the place you just visited provides its
unusual views. Down the hill, the pavilions such as
Seungjaejeong, Gwallamjeong, Pyeomusa, and Jondeokjeong
catch your eyes one after another.

First, settle yourself in front of Jondeokjeong. It was first built
in the 22nd year of King Injo's reign (1644). Its initial name was
Yukmyeonjeong (six-sided pavilion) since it is hexagonal. Later, the
name was changed into Jondeokjeong. The pavilion has dual
roofs topped with a pagoda- shaped decorative tile. The lower

Dual roofs of Jondeokjeong Pavilion

A Pair of dragons on the ceiling

Tablet with King Jeongjo's writings

roof is called an *eyelash roof*. Also, the main floor is propped up by dual columns a and narrow veranda is attached along its outside, all of which reveal the high status of the pavilion. Next to the pavilion lies a small stone bridge. Records show that a sundial was placed south of the bridge. Maybe the beautiful stone pedestal, demonstrating excellent carving skill, in front of the bridge was for the sundial.

Now take a look at the inside. The ceiling has a picture bearing a blue and a red dragon as a symbol of the high status of the building. On the northern wall hangs a tablet with writings of King Jeongjo which reads "All the streams in the world have moons reflected on them, but there is the only one moon in the sky. The moon in the sky is me, the king, and the

343

Jondeokjeong Pavilion in summer

streams are you, my subjects." The text aptly expresses the ruling
philosophy of reform-minded Jeongjo teeming with compassion
for his people and resolution for the complete restoration of
royal authority. He confidently made it clear that he would look
after all his people as the moon shines over all the streams, and
that anyone challenging the only moon, which means the king,
would never be forgiven. The king added to his subjects, "It is the

344

principle of the universe that the streams reflect the moon. That is, following me is only right and proper since it conforms to the principles of *Taegeuk* (太極: Supreme Ultimate), and *yin* and *yang*."

The pool north of Jondeokjeong is called Half-moon Pond. The pond does not allow lotus flowers grow in it because of the low water temperature. It might sound silly to say this, but it looks like a symbol that his political prowess did not let his officials dare to confront the king.

In 2009 the Epistles of King Jeongjo were released from which we got a glimpse of one side of his personality. The royal letters revealed a totally unsuspected relationship between the

Each side of Jondeokjeong shows different greenery of the Rear garden.

king and Sim Hwanji, his political opponent.

Seemingly, the king and Sim Hwanji were in confrontation with each other. As a matter of fact, though, they consulted with each other on every pending issue via secret letters. The king valued Sim as his close aide to conspire with or even to devise a scenario with in order to push his policy forward. As the tablet in the pavilion and the epistles with Sim Hwanji show, King Jeongjo was a far stronger monarch armed with a more precautious and tenacious nature than you think.

Ginko leaves dye the Half-moon Pond in golden colors.

Pyeomusa Pavilion

On the hill beside Jondeokjeong stands Pyeomusa (貶愚榭) Pavilion, which means vigilance against folly. Crown Prince Hyomyeong would read books at the pavilion. In front of the pavilion lie some slabstones where Joseon noblemen would practice their elegant and decent walking. It will be great fun to act out nobility's gait: walk with their toes out. Remember,

How about looking into deep down in your heart filled with greed and folly before Pyeomusa Pavilion?

Name plaque of Pyeomusa

however, that you should flap your arms and walk with a swagger much more than you imagine. That is because Joseon noblemen were wearing so many layers of clothes with wide sleeves and roomy pants that they could not keep their steps straight under the sway of clothes without flapping their arms and swaggering steps.

Slabstones for practicing nobility's elegant walking

349

Gwallamjeong Pavilion and Bandoji Pond

Gwallamjeong (觀纜亭) Pavilion is a fan-shaped pavilion and its other name was Seonjajeong (扇子亭) as was recorded in *Gunggwolji* (Book of Palaces) compiled in 1908. According to the *Painting of the Eastern Palaces* (東闕圖) that was created around 1827, there used to be three small ponds in a row: two square ponds as symbols of the earth and one round pond as a symbol of heaven. In addition, there was no pavilion like Gwallamjeong. Then Gwallamjeong and a gourd-shaped pond appeared on '✿ *Donggwol-dohyeong*', the *Map of the Eastern Palaces* that was made around 1908. That

---

✿ *Donggwol-dohyeong* : The *Map of the Eastern Palaces* (東闕圖形) depicts the Eastern Palaces (Changdeokgung and Changgyeonggung) via modern mapping techniques. It is assumed to have been produced around 1908. The map had all the structures placed on square grids (1.2cm long and 1.2cm wide), giving relatively precise size and shape of the palace buildings. Compared with the *Painting of the Eastern Palaces* made around 1827, you notice several buildings were destroyed and newly built. These two resources are mutually complementary of each other's shortcomings, and are being used as important sources for the restoration of Changdeokgung and Changgyeonggung.

Name plaque of Gwallamjeong is in the shape of plantain leaf.

means the vicinity of Gwallamjeong was redesigned during Emperor Gojong's reign.

The pavilion is uniquely fan-shaped. It is supported by six round columns on six cornerstones, with two out of six dipped into the pond. Its name plaque is also unique: a plantain leaf-shaped one. In addition, the pond around the pavilion has an unusual gourd-shaped curvedness. It is called Bandoji Pond, whose meaning is Peninsula Pond. That is because the pond, at first glance, looks like the Korean peninsula turned upside down. It is assumed that the change in the vicinity of Gwallamjeong took place with the intervention of Japanese Residency-General of

352

Korea during Emperor Gojong's rule.

There is something doubtful about the shape of the pond. Korean traditional landscaping included curve-lined ponds even though they were not so common. However, Bandoji leaves something more doubtful in that the atypical peninsula-typed pond like it is the first one. Given the circumstances of the early 20th century when Japan exerted a great influence all over the state affairs of Korea, they might have tried to brainwash Koreans that the Korean territory was just confined to the peninsula, not extended to Manchuria that Goguryeo, a strong warrior state during the Three Kingdoms period, kept under control. You may simply think the pond is just patterned after

Gwallamjeong is a fan-shaped pavilion.

the peninsula. Due to its reversed form of all things, though, uncomfortable feeling weighs down on Koreans.

In addition, Gwallamjeong is the only instance of fan-shaped pavilions until now as for architectural style. It is so unusual from the perspective of traditional landscaping that most architects, historians, and landscaping specialists have assumed that the pond and the pavilion were deliberately designed by Japanese authorities when they increasingly aggravated their power. Ironically, however, the stunning scenery here evokes admiration from tourists all the year round, nonchalant about the murky side of hidden history.

A pair of mandarin ducks is swimming like Darby and Joan on the Bandoji Pond

Gwallamjeong is clothed with fresh green leaves.

In Autumn Gwallamjeong reveals the most beautiful hues nature has ever generated.

Gwallamjeong looks so serene and calm while silence reigns on a snowy day.

Summer comes in through the pillars of Gwallamjeong.

Seungjaejeong Pavilion

On the hill across from Gwallamjeong stands Seungjaejeong (勝在亭) Pavilion. 'Seungjae' means outstanding scenery. When taking a walk along the path from Taeilmun to Seungjaejeong, looking at Pyeomusa, Jondeokjeong, and Gwallamjeong down below, the flavor from the forest trail and the rustling sounds from the fallen leaves couldn't be better. Since Seungjaejeong is standing atop a woody hill, you can enjoy a better view of the Gwallamjeong vicinity from Seungjaejeong. In front of the pavilion lies an oddly shaped stone. The stone with aesthetic value and the pavilion with classic beauty go together to create a superb landscape, which must have befitted someone who frequently visited the pavilion.

An oddly shaped stone before Seungjaejeong

Passing through Taeilmun Gate, you will catch sight of Seungjaejeong on the hill on your right.

Seungjaejeong seen through the pillars of Gwallamjeong

Walking by Aeryeonjeong and toward Bandoji,
the scenery will be all yours.

Jondeokjeong and Pyeomusa seen from the pond

15

Ongnyucheon Stream

Enjoying *Pungnyu*

Shall we take a walk along the secluded trail
towards Ongnyucheon Stream?

Chwigyujeong and Chwihanjeong Pavilions

In 1979, Ongnyucheon Stream (玉流川: Jade Stream) and its section of the Rear Garden of Changdeokgung Palace was placed a long sabbatical, being designated as a forbidden area since they were severely damaged from reckless opening to the public. It was a step taken to restore the ecology of the Rear Garden. Since then, a large number of people had looked forward to reopening the garden. At last, on May 1, 2004, the Rear Garden lifted the ban spanning 25 years and was opened to the public again in a special way of its own. At first, groups of 50 grown-ups older than 17 were allowed to enter the garden three times a day through online booking. However, the opening to the public had to be suspended due to the damage to the vicinity of the royal well that had been under the special protection of the palace management office. At the time just a month had passed since reopening, and the authorities concerned became hesitant between preservation and opening. After several twists and turns, luckily, the number of visitors to be admitted and that of guided tours to be offered have increased more and more.

Being seated deep inside the Rear Garden, Ongnyucheon

Chwigyujeong Pavilion

Stream and its vicinity are pretty well preserved. The layout of
the Ongnyucheon Stream section is acclaimed as the essence of
Joseon landscaping: beautiful harmony with nature and minimal
human touch. Moreover, the simple and modest appearance of
the garden structures is so amazing, given that they were

366

reserved for royal family members only.

Now, shall we cross the bridge and head north to get to Ongnyucheon Stream? At this point you are sure to feel a strong pull toward the secluded trail. Listen closely, and birds and winds from the royal grove will be whispering to you. Woodpeckers present their greetings to you by pecking at the tree bark on behalf of the royal grove that has arisen from 25-year-long slumbers.

Leaving the pavilion, you will turn right to the downhill path. The further down you go, the thicker and the deeper the surrounding forest gets. The first pavilion you meet in the

Chwihanjeong Pavilion

vicinity is 'Chwihanjeong (翠寒亭)', which was erected during King Sukjong's reign. It was the resting place for kings after they enjoyed the beautiful scenery of Jade Stream. 'Chwihan (翠寒)' coming from 'Changchwineunghan (蒼翠凌寒: Bluish-green pine trees despise the rigorous cold of winter) means 'bluish and cold'. As the name suggests, the vicinity was a dense forest of pine trees around 100 years ago. Then its vegetation has changed over the years and it was designated as a Zelkova tree Habitat in 1983.

Cross a narrow stone bridge behind Chwihanjeong, you will get to Soyojeong (逍遙亭) Pavilion. 'Soyo (逍遙)' means living free from worldly cares. King Sunjo said Soyojeong refreshed his body and mind even amid mounting pressure from state affairs.

The big rock in front of Soyojeong has King Injo's writing of Ongnyucheon engraved on it. King Sukjong's poem is engraved above the royal writing.

Soyojeong Pavilion

Scattering water flies from 300 feet above (飛流三百尺),

falling out of nine heavens afar (搖落九天來).

I see white rainbow spreading all around (看是白虹起)

and hear the thunder rumbling all over the valley (繡盛萬壑雷).

In the 14th year of King Injo's rule (1636), a water course was drawn to the back of the Soyoam Rock from Eungbong Peak (鷹峯: the guardian hill of Changdeokgung) and the whole topography including the valley was intactly adopted to build its neighborhood with minimal human touch. A U-shaped groove was cut on the broad flat rock to change the waterway to form a small waterfall. The king and his subjects enjoyed a special party

King Injo's writing and King Sukjong's poem

sending wine cups afloat along the water. When the wine cup stopped at any person, he was supposed to drink the wine and recite an impromptu poem. The scene truly shows how the Joseon literati enjoyed *pungnyu* (風流: literati's elegant and carefree way of enjoying arts and culture). King Jeongjo wrote a poem about the beautiful view of composing poetry with sending wine cups afloat:

370

Scattering water flies from 300 feet above (飛流三百尺)

Soyoyusang (逍遙流觴: floating wine cups at Soyojeong Pavilion). The poem is the fifth one of the 10 quadrains with seven-letter lines whose title is Ten Scenic Views of the Royal Grove (上林十景). They are included in King Jeongjo's anthology, *Hongjaejeonseo* (弘齋全書).

Getting to the waterfall at Soyoam Rock and reciting King Sukjong's poem, you have come face to face with metaphors and overstatements of Joseon poets and calligraphers, who

371

displayed their fascination with nature through rich sensitivity. To your disappointment, though, the waterfall looks really tiny compared to the phrase of 'Scattering water flies from 300 feet above (飛流三百尺).' I wonder whether your sensitivity paralyzed by ear-deafening heavy metal can recognize the thunderous sounds rumbling all over the valley. Also, I wonder if you are able to find the white rainbow spreading over the water only with the eyes of your heart, since you are already accustomed to glamorous and boisterous settings.

Jade Stream is dyeing the scattering water with autumn tints…

Soyojeong, Taegeukjeong, and Cheonguijeong are collectively called 'Three Pavilions of the Royal Grove' since they are noted for their scenic beauty in the Jade Stream vicinity. King Sukjong picked Taegeukjeong (太極亭) out of the three pavilions as the place kings would cultivate their moral culture. The present Taegeukjeong has only pillars with no windows, but hinges still remain on the pillars and the pavilion depicted on the *Painting*

Taegeuljeong Pavilion

374

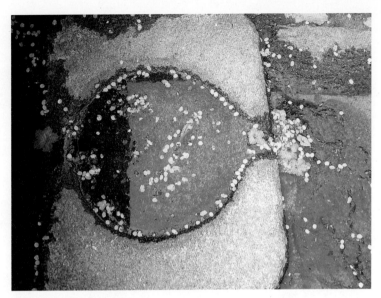

Taegeuk pattern in the small cistern

of the Eastern Palaces had windows. You can guess the king would be served food or refreshments at Taegeukjeong.

Between the pavilion and the royal well a small stone bridge is lying over the brook. If you take a close look at the small cistern, you will recognize the apparent *taegeuk* (☯) pattern engraved at the bottom. The current is drifting gently and then flowing lightly over the projection, which also makes you feel relaxed. The Royal well is being protected not by a wooden gazebo, but by a capstone topped with a grip resembling the hibiscus bud. The well seems to have been made during King Gojong's reign or Japanese Occupation since it is not found in

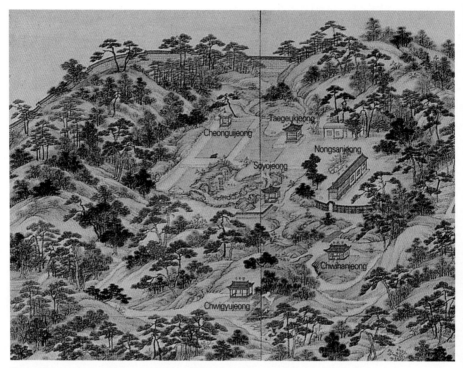

Ongnyucheon area in the *Painting of the Eastern Palaces*

the *Painting of the Eastern Palaces.* Please make sure you do not tread on the moss community around the well since it is now being protected as a Moss habitat.

Spring around Taegeukjeong and Cheonguijeong

Cheonguijeong is the only straw-thatched pavilion in the whole palace. 'Cheongui (清漪) means 'clear ripples'. In accordance with the Taoist idea of the round heaven and the square earth, its roof is round and its floor square.

The *Painting of the Eastern Palaces* portrays Taegeukjeong and Cheonguijeong lying beside the pond side by side and that the pond was before Cheonguijeong, not the rice paddy as you now see. Nowadays, the Changdeokgung Office is reenacting *Chingyeongnye* (親耕禮: Plow-in-person Ceremony) of former kings in a

Cheonguijeong built after a Taoist condept of a round *heaven and square earth*

The ceiling of Cheonguijeong is decorated with *dancheong* pattern

378

Every spring the rice planting is reenacted in the rice paddy of Cheonguijeong in a simple form of *Chingyeongnye.*

simple form with the participation of citizens and its staff. Although the harvest from the rice paddy is not so plentiful since the paddy is in the shade, passing down the legacy that the king tried to share everyday hardships with his people through conducting plowing and mowing in the rice paddy means a lot.

✿ **Plow-in-person Ceremony** (*Chingyeongnye*) : In late spring Joseon kings performed the Plow-in- person Ceremony to set an example of farming for his people. First, the king offered sacrifices at the Altar of Agriculture (先農壇) dedicated to two deities: one is the god of agriculture (神農氏: believed to have made the first farming tools) and the other the god of grain (后稷氏: said to have cultivated the first crop). Then the king demonstrated in person how to till the soil and plant seeds at the field placed south of the Altar. After the king worked the field with a plow pulled by two black oxen, the crown prince as well as officials and commoners took their turns to plow and plant. The ceremony was wrapped up with throwing a party for all the participants. Joseon was an agricultural society which attached lots of importance to the Plow-in-person Ceremony of the king and the In-person Sericulture Ceremony (親蠶禮) of the queen in an effort for the king and the queen to share men's labor of farming and women's work of weaving. Changgyeonggung Palace used to have some rice paddy on the premises. Rice seedlings were planted in the spring and ripened grains of rice were harvested in fall. Then the old thatched roof of Cheonguijeong could be replaced with new rice straws. Also, Changdeokgung Palace has several mulberry trees all over, which are the

trace of the In-person Sericulture Ceremony (親蠶禮) presided over by the queen. One of these trees was designated as a Natural Monument for its old age of some 400 years.

Summer at Cheonguijeong Pavilion

After looking around the Jade Stream, you can find Nongsanjeong (籠山亭) Pavilion facing east. The pavilion equipped with a room and a kitchen served food and beverage for the king when the king visited the Jade Stream. The Painting of the Eastern Palaces depicts that Nongsanjeong was surrounded with *chibyeong* (翠屏: quickset screen with bamboo frames) to the south and had a wooden bridge in the front.

Nongsanjeong Pavilion

In 1795 (the 19th year of King Jeongjo's rule) the king trained palanquin bearers to carry his mother in the palanquin all over the Rear Garden and treated them with food at Nongsanjeong. The training was a preliminary drill to take his mother, Lady Hyegyeonggung Hong, to Hwaseong more comfortably while she was traveling to the detached palace in Hwaseong Fortress. The year of 1795 was the year when not only his mother but his late father, Crown Prince Sado, turned 60. The king planned to celebrate his parents' sixtieth birthday at Hwaseong Fortress where his father was buried. So they had to take a long trip to Hwaseong.

While there are so many convenient means of transportation such as a car or a subway to get to Hwaseong from Seoul these days, back then they had to ride a horse, an ox-driven cart, or a palanquin carried by bearers. Of course, you are well aware of palanquin bearers' toil. They could take turns carrying the vehicle, though. On the other hand, passengers carried by sedan chair had a hard time enduring bumpy, rickety movements all the way down to their destination.

Taegeukjeong Pavilion and Cheonguijeong Pavilion seen from
Nongsanjeong Pavilion

❖ **Cheongsimjeong Pavilion** (淸心亭): It is seated to the left around halfway between the Jade Stream and the main gate. Cheongsimjewol (淸心霽月: Moon on a clear day at Cheongsimjeong) is the seventh scenic spot of Ten Scenic Views of the Royal Grove. The cistern in the front of the pavilion has a stone turtle engraved with Bingokji (氷玉池) in the king's hand writing.

❖ **Bingcheon Stream** (氷川, freezing stream): It is situated to the right on the way from Jade Stream down to Yeongyeongdang Residence. As the name indicates, the water is freezing cold enough to feel chilly even on hot summer days. The waterway extends through the western corridor of Yeongyeongdang to Jangnakmun Gate.

❖ **Neungheojeong Pavilion** (凌虛亭): It stands on the highest hill of the Rear Garden, northwest of Cheongsimjeong Pavilion. The tenth poem of *Ten Scenic Views of the Royal Grove* is *Neungheomoseol* (凌虛暮雪: Snowing in the evening at Neungheojeong Pavilion).

❖ **Darae, Siberian gooseberry**: It is planted deep inside the Rear Garden. It is assumed to be 660 years old or so. The trunk of the tree is so long that you cannot find the beginning and the end, and its endlessly tangled shape reminds us of intertwined dragons. The tree is designated as Korean Natural Monument No. 251.

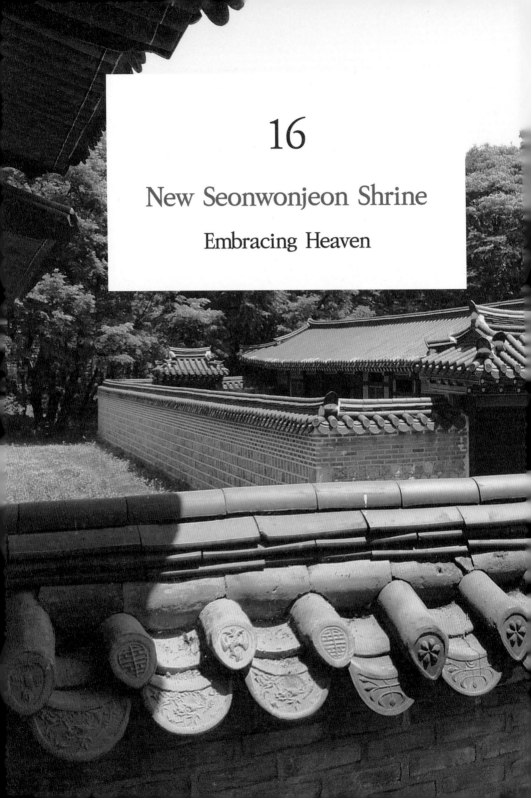

16

New Seonwonjeon Shrine

Embracing Heaven

New Seonwonjeon Shrine was newly erected in the place where Daebodan Altar had originally been set up.

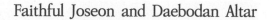

Faithful Joseon and Daebodan Altar

Changdeokgung Palace has two Seonwonjeon Shrines on the premises: One is New Seonwonjeon that was newly erected in the place where Daebodan Altar had been seated, and the other is Old Seonwonjeon that still remains in its original location as an empty building. That is because the Japanese authorities removed Daebodan Altar that had been lying northwest in the palatial compound and set up a new shrine on the site in 1921. The initial altar built in 1704 during King Sukjong's rule was dedicated to Emperor Wanli (萬曆帝) of Ming China who sent reinforcement forces to Joseon during the Japanese invasion of 1592. Afterwards, in 1749 during King Yeongjo's reign the spirit tablets of the first and the last emperors of Ming China were also enshrined in the altar, and all three Chinese emperors were offered sacrifices.

Peony pattern engraved on the stone balustrade of the platform staircase in New Seonwonjeon

Sukgyeongmun Gate

Daebodan' marked as Hwangdan (皇壇) on the *Painting of the Eastern Palaces* literally means returning a favor. In the year of 1704 King Sukjong established Daebodan, marking the 60th anniversary of the Ming dynasty defeat by the Qing dynasty. The Joseon dynasty whose ruling philosophy was neo-Confucianism had a good reason to erect the altar as a way to repay an obligation to Ming China. Also, Joseon might want to reclaim its pride as *Sojunghwa* (小中華: its literal translation is little China in alignment with Sinocentrism), since Joseon had been deeply humiliated by Qing China's invasion in 1636. After Ming China went out of existence, the small country Joseon considered itself succeeding to Ming

390

China as the global epicenter. When the altar was installed in 1704, mainland China was under the control of Qing with the Ming dynasty already wiped out. From then until 1908 (during Emperor Sunjong's reign), for as long as 200 years, Joseon kings had held the ancestral ceremonies for Ming emperors with faithful courteousness.

Then Japanese authorities could hardly afford to leave the altar intact there since the altar could remind Joseon people of the Japanese invasions in the 16th century. In1921 the Japanese Government-general tore down the altar and erected New Seonwonjeon Shrine under the pretext that Seonwonjeon needed to be relocated.

New Seonwonjeon Shrine is the last-built portrait hall, which upheld to the last the great tradition of enshrining royal portraits and offering sacrifices. The portraits of successive kings kept at Seonwonjoen of Deoksugung and of Old Seonwonjeon of Chandeokgung were all transferred to New Seonwonjeon. Unfortunately, most of them were lost in fires during the Korean War. In 1950 when the war broke out, the whole collection of 48 portraits of 12 kings was moved to Busan, where the storage housing the royal portraits caught fires. New Seonwonjeon has some annex buildings such as Uihyojeon Hall, Jesil Office, and Sujiksa Checkpoint.

New Seonwonjeon Shrine is the royal portrait enshrining hall that was established most recently of all the portrait halls.

Gwaegungjeong and Mongdapjeong
Pavilions of *Bugyeong*

Hullyeondogam (the Military Training Command) also called *Hunguk*, was in charge of defending the capital of the Joseon dynasty. *Bugyeong* (北營, Northern Camp) was its headquarters and Gwaegungjeong Pavilion (掛弓亭) seems to have been a site for arrow shooting drills. '*Gwaegung* (掛弓)' means drawing a bow to let fly an arrow.

Gwaegungjeong

Jeong Yak-yong (who was a prominent scholar-official in the 18th century and now is respected as one of the greatest scholars and writers of the Joseon dynasty) was locked up in Bugyeong to be engaged in exhausting archery training under King Jeongjo's order when he worked for the *Gyujanggak* Library.

King Jeongjo had *Gyujanggak* officials shoot arrows ten rounds of sun (50 shots/ 1 *sun* is equivalent to five shots) at Chundangdae Field of the Rear Garden in 1791. Then he ordered some officials hitting the target less than four times to practice shooting 20 rounds of sun (100 shots) every day.

The king himself was excellent at archery. The first article dated November 26th, 1792 from *King Jeongjo's Annals* says that the king went on an archery tour to Chundangdae Field many times and hit the target 49 times out of 10 rounds of *sun* (50 shots). King Jeongjo shot arrows and hit the mark successively with unerring aim, turned to his officials, and said, "Making the target only 49 out of 50 shots suffices me these days. What I intend is to make myself fall short of perfection."

The king would chide some scholar-officials that were good only at literary skills but poor at archery, telling them the main prop of Joseon needed to be masters in both arts of the pen and the sword. He announced that he would get those officials that turned out to be unskilled archers locked up in the northern camp for shooting training, and that they would have to

The rock in the back of Mongdapjeong is engraved with an epigraph of 夢踏亭

discharge arrows 20 rounds of *sun* (100 shots) every day. Those who could hit the target at least once per every sun were supposed to be released.

Under the king's direction, Jeong Yak-yong and his party started shooting drills. At first, their records were far from being satisfactory. They were so clumsy at using bows and arrows that they had their bows broken, their arrows bent, and their horn rings for the thumb fallen off. They also got their hands blistered and their forearms swollen up. Moreover, their horse riding skills were awkward enough to be laughed at by on-lookers. Before long, though, they became so adept at handling archery tools that many of them were able to hit the target three times out of a *sun* (five shots). Then the king cut in half their mandatory shooting rounds of sun to 10 rounds (50 shots) and allowed them to engage themselves in studying Confucian classics in their spare time. It was not until 10 days later that Jeong Yak-yong and his party won recognition of their improved archery skills and were finally released from the northern camp. The first article dated November 26th, 1792 from *King Jeongjo's Annals*:

395

Your majesty shot arrows and hit the bull's eye successively. Then, he turned to officials and said, "Making the target only 49 out of 50 shots suffices me these days. What I intend is to make myself fall short of perfection." Afterward, he shot another arrow and then let fly four arrows to the bull's eye, ending up with making the mark 14 times out of three rounds of sun (15 shots). And the king aimed at smaller target to hit the bull's eye three times out of a sun (five shots). Furthermore, he aimed at the small club to hit the target three times of a sun. The king had officers and soldiers all over the northern camp as well as Gyujanggak officials treated with food.

The above article from *King Jeongjo's Annals* shows King Jeongjo was an excellent archer and that he nearly forced his officials to acquire not only literary arts but also martial arts. The king seems to have taken archery tours so often to Chundangdae Field and shown off his archery skills. As for Jeong Yak-yong who had no interest and skill in military arts, he seemed to have been in big trouble doing archery drills.

Right behind Gwaegungjeong Pavilion standing on the northern hill of Mongdapjeong Pavilion, the fence of Jungang High Shool

Mongdapjeong Pavilion shaded with greenery.

The pond in front of Mongdapjeong makes the scenery more attractive.

sits quite closely. Gwaegungjeong no longer sees arrows shot by archers, but gets some balls tossed over the fence from time to time by footballers of Jungang High School.

Mongdapjeong belonged to *Bugyeong* (Northern Camp). King Sukjong endowed the pavilion with the name of Mongdapjeong since the king had a dream in which he ascended to the pavilion. 'Mongdap (夢踏)' means treading the path in a dream. The rocks in the back and the pond in the front make the scenery more dreamlike.

⊙ The Map of Changdeokgung Palace

The UNESCO World Cultural Heritage Site,
Changdeokgung Palace

Ten Scenic Views of Changdeokgung Palace

How will your tour around Changdeokgung be remembered? Many looks of the palace are sure to be kept in your memory. I hope the memory will recur to your mind just like a picture. I suggest you draw Ten Scenic Views of Changdeokgung Palace in your heart.

Ten Scenic Views of palace building complex

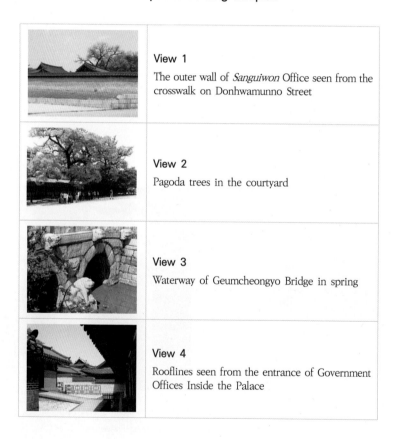

View 1

The outer wall of *Sanguiwon* Office seen from the crosswalk on Donhwamunno Street

View 2

Pagoda trees in the courtyard

View 3

Waterway of Geumcheongyo Bridge in spring

View 4

Rooflines seen from the entrance of Government Offices Inside the Palace

View 5

The *ilwoldam* wall spreading at the back of Injeongjeon Hall

View 6

Snow-covered pine tree viewed through the decorative wooden panels of Huijeongdang porch

View 7

Huiuru Pavilion in apricot blossoms in April

View 8

Hongmaehwa (red winter plum) next to Jasimun Gate

View 9

The snow-capped wall of Nakseonjae

View 10

Flower-patterned brick walls and Manwolmun Gate of the rear garden of Nakseonjae

Ten scenic views of Rear Garden

View 1

The path leading to Rear Garden is clothed in fresh green leaves.

View 2

Buyongji Pond is shaded with summer greenery.

View 3

I hear drizzling spring rain, sitting on the floor of Yeonghwadang Hall

View 4

Aeryeonjeong Pavilion and Aeryeonji Pond dyed with crimson foliage

View 5

Listening to *daegeum* (traverse bamboo flute) tune under the moon on a clear day.

	**View 6** *Naeoedam* wall in the Yeongyeongdang Residence
	**View 7** Seungjaejeong Pavilion viewed in autumn through the decorative wooden panels of Gwallamjeong Pavilion
	**View 8** The rustling sound of fallen leaves on the hill at the back of Yeongyeongdang Residence
	**View 9** Hearing waterfall falling from 300 feet above scattering all over at Ongnyucheon Stream
	**View 10** Feeling a breath of spring at Cheonguijeong Pavilion

The Genealogy of the Joseon Dynasty

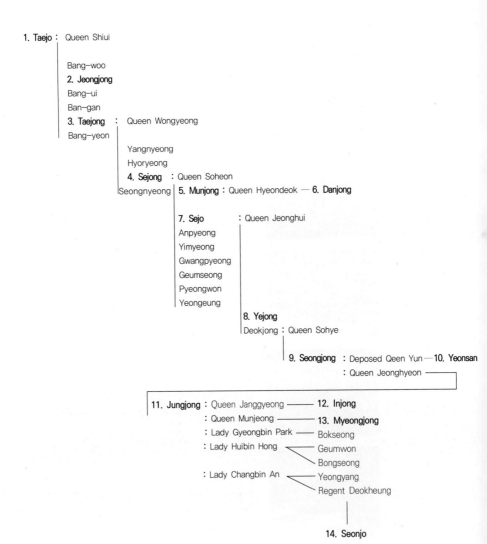

1. **Taejo** : Queen Shiui

   Bang—woo
   2. Jeongjong
   Bang—ui
   Ban—gan
   3. Taejong : Queen Wongyeong
   Bang—yeon

   Yangnyeong
   Hyoryeong
   4. Sejong : Queen Soheon
   Seongnyeong | **5. Munjong** : Queen Hyeondeok — **6. Danjong**

   7. Sejo : Queen Jeonghui
   Anpyeong
   Yimyeong
   Gwangpyeong
   Geumseong
   Pyeongwon
   Yeongeung

   8. Yejong
   Deokjong : Queen Sohye

   9. Seongjong : Deposed Qeen Yun — **10. Yeonsan**
   : Queen Jeonghyeon

   11. Jungjong : Queen Janggyeong ——— **12. Injong**
   : Queen Munjeong ——— **13. Myeongjong**
   : Lady Gyeongbin Park —— Bokseong
   : Lady Huibin Hong ⟨ Geumwon
   Bongseong
   : Lady Changbin An ⟨ Yeongyang
   Regent Deokheung

   14. Seonjo

Seonjo : Queen Uiin
      : Queen Inmok ——————— Great Prince Yeongchang
      : Lady Gongbin Kim — Imhae
                    15. Gwanghae
      : Lady Inbin Kim — Uian
                   Sinseong
                   Jeongwon ——— **16. Injo** : Queen Innryeol
                   Uichang
                                Crown Prince Sohyeon
                                17. Hyojong : Queen Inseon
                                Inpyeong
                                Yongseong   **18. Hyeonjong** : Queen Myeongseong
                                                  19. Sukjong : Queen Ingyeong
                                                         : Queen Inhyeon
                                                         : Queen Inwon
                                         : Lady Huibin Jang —**20. Gyeongjong**
                                         : Lady Sukbin Choi —**21. Yeongjo**

. Yeongjo : Queen Jeongseong
         : Queen Jeongsun
: Lady Jeongbin Yi —— Crown Prince Hyojang
: Lady Yeongbin Yi ———— Crown Prince Sado : Crown Princess Hyebin Hong ——— **22. Jeongjo** : Queen Hyoui
                                              : Lady Uibin Seong ———— Crown Prince Munhyo
                                              : Lady Subin Park —— **23. Sunjo** : Queen Sunwon
                                         Crown Prince Hyomyeong : Queen Sinjeong
                                                   24. Heonjong
: Lady Sukbin Im — Euneon — Regent Jeongye — **25. Cheoljong**
                Eunsin — Namyeon — Regent Heungseon : Prince Consort Min
: Lady Gyeongbin Park — Eunjeon
                                             26. Gojong

26. Gojong : Empress Myeongseong — **27. Sunjong** : Empress Sunmyeonghyo
                                            : Empress Sunjeonghyo
                          : Lady Gwiin Eom — King Yeongchin
                          : Lady Gwiin Yi — King Wanchin
                          : Lady Gwiin Jang — King Uichin
                          : Lady Gwiin Jeong — Wu
                          : Lady Gwiin Yang — Princess Deokhye

A Chronological Table of Changdeokgung Palace History

Year	Regnal year of King	Events
1392	King Taejo 1	The Joseon Dynasty was founded.
1394	King Taejo 3	The Capital was moved to Hanyang (current Seoul).
1399	King Jeongjong 1	The Capital was moved to Gaegyeong (current Gaeseong).
1404	King Taejong 4	The construction of the secondary palace was begun in Hyanggyo-dong, Hanyang.
1405	King Taejong 5	The secondary palace was named 'Changdeokgung' It had 74 square-*kan* outer court area and 118 square-*kan* inner court area.
1406	King Taejong 6	Gwangyeonnu and Haeonjeong were built in the palace.
1411	King Taejong 11	Geumcheongyo Bridge was constructed.
1412	King Taejong 12	Donhwamun Gate was constructed as the main gate of Changdeokgung.
1462	King Sejo 8	The formation of the rear garden area was begun in full scale by removing the civil residential areas in the northwestern part of the rear garden, and by relocating the walls to expand the plottage of the palace. The boundary of the rear garden was fixed.
1496	King Yeonsan 2	Sungmundang was rebuilt and renamed as 'Huijeongdang.'
1592	King Seonjo 25	Due to the outbreak of Japanese Invasion, Gyeongbokgung, Changdeokgung, and Changgyeonggung were burned down.

1610	King Gwanghae 2	The burnt buildings in Changdeokgung including Seonjeongjeon, Daejojeon, Huijeongdang and others were reconstructed, and thereby Changdeokgung began to function as the main palace.
1616	King Gwanghae 8	Restored Changgyeonggung Palace.
1623	King Gwanghae 15	Due to the Coup of King Injo to dethrone King Gwanghae, major buildings in Changdeokgung were destroyed by fire.
1624	King Injo 2	Due to the Revolt of Yi Gwal, Changdeokgung and Changgyeonggung were destroyed by fire. King Injo moved to Gyeongdeokgung, current Gyeonghuigung.
1632	King Injo 10	The king moved to Changdeokgung.
1633	King Injo 11	The restoration of Changgyeonggung was completed, and the king moved to Changgyeonggung.
1636	King Injo 14	Formed Ongnyucheon Stream area in the rear garden. Pavilions including Taeguekjeong, Cheonguijeong, Soyojeong were built in the rear garden. Nakminjeong, Chwigyujeong, and Simchujeong Pavilions were constructed, too. Due to the Invasion of Qing China, the king took a refuge in Namhansanseong Fortress
1637	King Injo 15	The king returned to Changgyeonggung Palace.
1647	King Injo 25	Changdeokgung was restored.
1688	King Sukjong 13	Cheongsimjeong Pavilion was built to the north of Pyeomusa. Bingokji Pond was formed in the southern yard of Cheongsimjeong Pavilion.
1690	King Sukjong 15	Sajeonggibigak (Stele Shed of Four Wells) was built on the site of Sulseonggak.
1704	King Sukjong 30	Daebodan Altar was established in honor of Emperor Wan-li of Ming China to repay his favor of sending reinforcement forces for Joseon during the

		Japanese Invasion of 1592.
1707	King Sukjong 33	Taeksujae Hall (Buyongjeong Pavilion) was built by the pond in front of Juhamnu Pavilion.
1744	King Yeongjo 20	A fire broke out in the Royal Secritariat's Office, and the east and the west corridor buildings of Injeongjeon Hall were burned.
1776	the year King Jeongjo was crowned	Gyujanggak Library was established in the rear garden.
1777	King Jeongjo 1	The stone rank markers were set up in the courtyard of Injeongjeon Hall.
1782	King Jeongjo 6	Junghuidang Hall was constructed.
1785	King Jeongjo 9	Sugangjae Hall was built.
1803	King Sunjo 3	Injeongjeon Hall was destroyed by fire, and was rebuilt in 1804.
1811	King Sunjo 11	Due to a fire in Yemungwan and Hyangsil, many books and objects were burned.
1824	King Sunjo 24	Gyeongbokjeon Hall to the rear of Injeongjeon was lost by fire.
1827	King Sunjo 27	Yeongyeongdang Residence was constructed by Crown Prince Hyomyeong.
1827~30	King Sunjo 27~30	The *Painting of the Eastern Palaces* was made.
1833	King Sunjo 33	Due to a big fire in the inner court area, Daejojeon, Huijeongdang, and their corridor buildings wer burned, and they were rebuilt in 1834.
1847	King Heonjong 13	Nakseonjae Complex was constructed.
1857	King Cheoljong 8	Injeongjeon Hall was completely taken apart and repaired in the 53rd year since it was restored in

		1804.
1863	the year King Gojong was crowned	King Gojong was crowned at Injeongjeon Hall of Changdeokgung.
1884	King Gojong 21	Due to the outbreak of Gapsin Coup, the Enlightenment Party took King Gojong to Gwanmulheon Hall in Changdeokgung.
1897	Emperor Gojong 1	King Gojong declared foundation of Great Han Empire, and was crowned as Emperor Gojong.
1905	Emperor Gojong 5	Japan-Korea Treaty of 1905 was signed, thereby the diplomatic sovereignty of Joseon was deprived of by Japan.
1908	Emperor Sunjong 2	Injeongjeon Hall was repaird and Jinseonmun Gate was demolished.
1910	Emperor Sunjong 4	The last cabinet meeting of Great Han Empire was held in Heungbokjeon Hall of Changdeokgung.
1917		A big fire of unknown cause broke out at Daejojeon, and the most of the buildings in the inner court area including Daejojeon were burned. Emperor Sunjong and his empress took a refuge in the Yeongyeongdang Residence in the Rear Garden.
1920		Most of the buildings in the inner court area of Gyeongbokgung Palace including Gangnyeongjeon and Gyotaejeon were dismantled to rebuild the burnt buildings in Changdeokgung with the materials taken apart from Gyeongbokgung. The burnt buildings in Changdeokgung including Daejojeon, Huijeongdang, Heungbokheon, Gyeonghungak and Hamwonjeon were rebuilt.
1926		Emperor Sunjong deceased in Daejojeon Hall.
1989		Princess Deokhye passed away in Sugangjae Hall. The last Imperial Crown Princess Uimin (Yi Bang-ja) of the Great Han Empire, deceased in Nakseonjae Hall.

409

1994~97		The refurbishment of the Nakseonjae Complex and the vicinity was carried out.
1995~97		Donhwamun Gate was taken apart and restored. The *woldae* (stone platform) of Donhwamun was also restored.
1995~99		The outer corridor buildings of Injeongjeon Hall were rebuilt and restored including Jinseonmun and Sukjangmun Gates.
1997		Changdeokgung was designated as a Wold Heritage by UNESCO.

References

Internets

Korean Britanica, http://www.britannica.co.kr/
Kyujanggak Institute for Korean Studies in Seoul National University,
    http://e-kyujanggak.snu.ac.kr
Institute for the Translation of Korean Classic, http://www.minchu.or.kr
The Annals of the Joseon Dynasty, http://sillok.history.go.kr
The Daily Records of Royal Secretariat of Joseon Dynasty, http://sjw.history.go.kr
Wikipedia, http://ko.wikipedia.org/

Korean Books

Changdeokgung 600 Years (in Korean). Changdeokgung Office, Cultural Heritage
    Administration of Korea, 2005.
Choe, Jong-deok. *Joseon ui Chamgunggwol Changdeokgung.* Nulwa, 2006.
Cultural Heritage Administration. *Gunggwol ui Hyeonpan gua Juryeon 1:
    Gyeongbokgung.* Suryusanbang, 2007.
_____. *World Heritage in Korea* (in Korean). Nulwa, 2007.
_____. *Sunan ui Munhwaje.* Nulwa, 2009.
_____. *The royal palaces and royal shrine of Joseon* (in Korean), Nulwa, 2010.
Gilsang (Best wishes: Auspicious symbols in Chinese art) (in Korean). The National
    Museum of Korea, 2012.
Gunggwolji. Seoul Teukbyeolsi History Publishing Committee, 2nd Edition, 2000.
Gunggwolji 1: Gyeongbokgung, Changdeokgung. Seoul Study Center, 1994.
Gunggwolji 2: Changgyeonggung, Gyeonghuigung, Doseongji. Seoul Study Center,
    1994.
Her, Gyun. *Jeontong Misul ui Sojae wa Sangjing* (in Korean). Kyobomungo, 2001.
Hong, Soon-min. *Wuri Gunggwol Yiyagi.* Cheongnyeonsa, 1999.
Jang, Heon-deok. *Mokjo Geonchuk ui Guseong.* Korean Cultural Heritage
    Foundation, 2006.
Jeong, Jae-hun, et al. *Soswaewon.* Daewonsa, 2002.
Jeong, Yeon-sik. *Ilsang euro Bon Joseon Sidae Yiyagi.* Cheongnyeonsa, 2001.
Kang, Gyeong-seon, et al. *Yiyagiga Yitneun Gyeongbokgung Nadeuri.* Yeoksanet,
    2000.

411

Kim, Dong-hyeon. *Seoul ui Gunggwol Geonchuk*. Sigongsa, 2002.

Kim, Jae-won. *Gyeongbokgung Yahwa*. Tamgudang, 2000.

Kim, Mun-shik and Byeong-ju Shin. *Joseon Wangsil Girok Munhwa ui Got*, Uigwue. Dolbegae, 2005.

Kim, Wang-jik. *Algi Shiwun Hanguk Geonchuk Yongeo Sajeon*. Dongnyeok, 2007.

Kim, Yeong-mo. *Algi Shiwun Jeontong Jogyeong Siseol Sajeon*. Dongnyeok, 2012.

Kim, Yeong-sang. *Seoul 600 Years* (in Korean). Hangukilbosa, 1990.

National Research Institute of Cultural Heritage. *Haksuljosabogo vol 19: Gyeongbokgung Taewonjeonji*. Korea Cultural Heritage Foundation, 1998.

Park, Hong-gap. *Haneul wieneun Sagawani Itsoida*. Garamgihwoek, 1999.

Park, Sang-jin. *Gunggwol ui Wurinamu*. Nulwa, 2001.

Park, Yeong-gyu. *Hangwon euro Ingneun Joseon Wangjo Sillok*. Deulnyeok, 1996.

Seoul Teukbyeolsi. *History Publishing Committee*. Cultural Properties of Seoul (in Korean), 2011.

_____. *Seoul 600 Year History* (in Korean). Munhwasajeokpyeon, 1987.

Shin, Eung-su. *Gunggwol ui Hyeonpan gua Juryeon 1: Gyeongbokgung Geunjeongjeon Jungsugi, Gyeongbokgung Geunjeongjeon*. Hyeonamsa, 2005.

Shin, Myeong-ho. *Joseon ui Wang*. Garamgihwoek, 1998.

Shin, Myeong-ho. *Joseon Royal Court Culture: Ceremonial and Daily Life*. Translated by Timothy V. Atkinson. Dolbegae Publishers, 2002

The National Museum of Korea Collection Yuri Geonpan, Gunggwol. The National Museum of Korea, 2007.

Yi, Sun-wu. *Geudeul un Jeongmal Joseon eul Sarang Hatseulga*. Haneuljae, 2005.

Yu, Bon-ye and Gwon Tae-ik, trans. *Hangyeongjiryak*. Tamgudang, 1975.

Yun, Jang-seop. *The History of Korean Architecture* (in Korean). Dongmyeongsa, 1981.

Korean Thesis

Jang, Yeong-gi. "Joseon Sidae Gunggwol Jangshik Giwa ui Giwon gwa Uimi." Master's thesis, Gukmin University, 2004.

Hong, Soon-min. "The management of royal palaces and the changes of 'the dual palace managing system' in Choson dynasty." Ph.D. diss., Seoul National University, 1996.